Foundations for Architecting Data Solutions

Managing Successful Data Projects

Ted Malaska and Jonathan Seidman

Beijing · Boston · Farnham · Sebastopol · Tokyo

Foundations for Architecting Data Solutions

by Ted Malaska and Jonathan Seidman

Published by O'Reilly Media, Inc., 1005 Gravenstein Highway North, Sebastopol, CA 95472.

O'Reilly books may be purchased for educational, business, or sales promotional use. Online editions are also available for most titles (*http://oreilly.com/safari*). For more information, contact our corporate/institutional sales department: 800-998-9938 or *corporate@oreilly.com*.

Editors: Nicole Tache and Michele Cronin	**Indexer:** Judy McConville
Production Editor: Nicholas Adams	**Interior Designer:** David Futato
Copyeditor: Octal Publishing, Inc.	**Cover Designer:** Karen Montgomery
Proofreader: Sharon Wilkey	**Illustrator:** Rebecca Demarest

September 2018:   First Edition

Revision History for the First Edition

2018-08-29:   First Release

See *http://oreilly.com/catalog/errata.csp?isbn=9781492038740* for release details.

978-1-492-03874-0

[LSI]

Table of Contents

Preface

If you're reading this book, you already know that there have been dramatic shifts in the data management landscape in recent years. We've seen a shift from third-party, proprietary solutions to new, open source distributed data systems. Of course, the common term used to refer to these newer solutions is "big data" (a term we find to be less and less useful), but it's important to note that many of the earlier proprietary systems utilize distributed architectures that can store and process large volumes of data. Although we can apply these proprietary solutions and the newer open source solutions to solve many of the same problems, there are some distinct differences that have contributed to the growth of the newer systems. This includes not just the economies of the open source approach, but also technology approaches that facilitate the implementation of many applications that are challenging with previous solutions.

Along with the growth of these systems, we've seen a corresponding growth in books, articles, training, conferences, and so on dedicated to help you, the practitioner, use these systems, so it's reasonable to ask why yet another book on this "big data" stuff? To quote a cliché, we think the answer is that it becomes easy to miss the forest for the trees. Most of these materials focus on low-level details such as implementing applications using distributed processing engines like MapReduce or Spark or applying advanced algorithms to perform data analysis. Others focus on higher-level architectural considerations; for example, *Hadoop Application Architectures* (O'Reilly), coauthored by the authors of this book.

The gap that we see is a perspective that takes an even wider view; in other words, what steps need to be taken to ensure successful data projects in this new landscape, from planning to execution? While developing the expertise in the architectures and component systems is critical, there are larger considerations that are equally important to your data projects, and these considerations can often be lost in the excitement of exploring new technologies.

These considerations include things like the following:

- Ensuring that you understand your problem
- Selecting software solutions that fit your use case
- Addressing project risk
- Building teams to successfully deliver projects
- Ensuring the implementation of robust, maintainable architectures and solutions as your project progresses

If you're an experienced software development practitioner, these considerations might sound very familiar, as they should. It's absolutely true that managing successful modern data projects requires many of the same processes as other software development projects. However, these new software systems and architectures require a new set of knowledge and considerations when developing projects. For example, evaluating software in an open source world can be very different from selecting proprietary solutions. Our intention is not to provide another book on managing software projects, but rather provide guidelines for applying sound project management and development practices to modern data solutions.

Who This Book Is For

This book is targeted at folks in an organization who are making decisions about data management projects and implementing those projects, such as the following:

- CxOs such as chief information officers or chief technology officers responsible for high-level decision making in an organization
- Project and product managers responsible for delivering data projects
- Lead architects, technical leads, and developers tasked with developing data projects

Again, we're not trying to provide you with the detailed knowledge to implement applications using specific components; instead, we provide a framework for understanding the basis of successful modern data projects. We want you to come away with the knowledge required to successfully navigate projects and make the decisions required to deliver data projects that provide real value to users.

Navigating This Book

Each chapter in this book addresses a different topic in data project management. It's not necessary to read through the entire book, because most chapters can stand on their own. However, before undertaking a new project, it would be helpful to read Chapter 1 through Chapter 3.

The following describes all of the chapters in this book:

- Chapter 1, *Key Data Project Types and Considerations* begins with an overview of the three major data project use cases and provides a list of items for each use case type that are important to consider before undertaking a project. This is a good place to start before undertaking a new data project.

- Chapter 2, *Evaluating and Selecting Data Management Solutions* provides guidelines for selecting technology solutions in this new world of distributed, open source software. This will also be a very useful chapter if you're starting on a data project, or just getting started in this space.

- Chapter 3, *Managing Risk in Data Projects* discusses project risk and how to manage it. Managing risk is an important activity in any software project, and implementing large data projects adds some unique aspects that need to be managed to ensure success.

- Chapter 4, *Interface Design* discusses the design and implementation of interfaces in your systems. Defining effective abstractions and contracts is crucial to creating maintainable and scalable systems, so this chapter provides some guidelines based on our experience implementing large data projects.

- Chapter 5, *Distributed Storage Systems* covers distributed storage systems. Data storage is a core component of any data system, and this chapter provides a breakdown of some commonly available distributed storage systems. More important, it provides a framework for evaluating systems.

- Chapter 6, *The Meta of Enterprise Data* covers metadata management. This is another critically important but often overlooked aspect of building systems that manage and process data.

- Chapter 7, *Ensuring Data Integrity* discusses data integrity. This is another important aspect of building data systems that needs to be planned for from project inception. Ensuring the integrity and lineage of data becomes more challenging and critical when building systems that store large volumes of data with multiple formats.

- Chapter 8, *Data Processing* discusses frameworks for performing distributed processing of data. The ability to process and analyze the data in your system is of course another crucial aspect to building systems that provide value. Similar to the storage chapter, this chapter provides a framework for understanding available systems and performing evaluations to determine which ones are suitable for your use cases.

Conventions Used in This Book

The following typographical conventions are used in this book:

Italic

> Indicates new terms, URLs, email addresses, filenames, and file extensions.

`Constant width`

> Used for program listings, as well as within paragraphs to refer to program elements such as variable or function names, databases, data types, environment variables, statements, and keywords.

> This element signifies a general note.

Using Code Examples

This book is here to help you get your job done. In general, if example code is offered with this book, you may use it in your programs and documentation. You do not need to contact us for permission unless you're reproducing a significant portion of the code. For example, writing a program that uses several chunks of code from this book does not require permission. Selling or distributing a CD-ROM of examples from O'Reilly books does require permission. Answering a question by citing this book and quoting example code does not require permission. Incorporating a significant amount of example code from this book into your product's documentation does require permission.

We appreciate, but do not require, attribution. An attribution usually includes the title, author, publisher, and ISBN. For example: "*Foundations for Architecting Data Solutions* by Ted Malaska and Jonathan Seidman (O'Reilly). Copyright 2018 Ted Malaska and Jonathan Seidman, 978-1-492-03874-0."

If you feel your use of code examples falls outside fair use or the permission given above, feel free to contact us at *permissions@oreilly.com*.

O'Reilly Safari

Safari (formerly Safari Books Online) is a membership-based training and reference platform for enterprise, government, educators, and individuals.

Members have access to thousands of books, training videos, Learning Paths, interactive tutorials, and curated playlists from over 250 publishers, including O'Reilly Media, Harvard Business Review, Prentice Hall Professional, Addison-Wesley Professional, Microsoft Press, Sams, Que, Peachpit Press, Adobe, Focal Press, Cisco Press, John Wiley & Sons, Syngress, Morgan Kaufmann, IBM Redbooks, Packt, Adobe Press, FT Press, Apress, Manning, New Riders, McGraw-Hill, Jones & Bartlett, and Course Technology, among others.

For more information, please visit *http://oreilly.com/safari*.

How to Contact Us

Please address comments and questions concerning this book to the publisher:

O'Reilly Media, Inc.
1005 Gravenstein Highway North
Sebastopol, CA 95472
800-998-9938 (in the United States or Canada)
707-829-0515 (international or local)
707-829-0104 (fax)

We have a web page for this book, where we list errata, examples, and any additional information. You can access this page at *http://bit.ly/foundations-for-architecting-data-solutions*.

To comment or ask technical questions about this book, send email to *bookquestions@oreilly.com*.

For more information about our books, courses, conferences, and news, see our website at *http://www.oreilly.com*.

Find us on Facebook: *http://facebook.com/oreilly*

Follow us on Twitter: *http://twitter.com/oreillymedia*

Watch us on YouTube: *http://www.youtube.com/oreillymedia*

Acknowledgments

Many people provided invaluable feedback and support while we wrote this book, especially Mark Grover, Kevin O'Dell, and Steven Totman, who provided their time and expertise to review content. These reviewers helped us out and greatly improved the quality of this book; any mistakes that remain are our own.

We'd like to thank our O'Reilly editors Nicole Tache and Michele Cronin for helping shepherd this book to completion. We also want to thank the folks at O'Reilly Media who provided help and support throughout the development of this book.

Our apologies to those whom we may have mistakenly omitted from this list.

CHAPTER 1

Key Data Project Types and Considerations

The basis for any successful data project is a clear understanding of what you're tasked to build and then understanding the major items that you need to consider in order to design a solid solution. We categorize data projects into three types that from our experience will typify many data projects. This categorization then allows us to explore the primary items we need to consider before starting on implementation. Not every project will fall neatly into one of these categories, and some projects might straddle these categories, but we feel that these project types will provide a useful framework for understanding your data use cases.

In this chapter, we begin by describing these major project types, followed by a description of the main items to consider, in general, for implementing solutions. We then take a deeper dive into these considerations for each project type.

Major Data Project Types

Let's begin by describing the three project types that we use to categorize data projects:

Data pipelines and data staging
> We can think of these as Extract, Transform, and Load (ETL)–type projects; in other words, these are projects that involve the collection, staging, storage, modeling, and so on of datasets. These are essentially projects that provide the basis for performing subsequent analysis and processing of data.

Data processing and analysis
> These are projects that end in providing some kind of actionable value. This might be the creation of reports, creation and execution of machine learning models, and so forth.

Applications

A data framework that's meant to support live operational needs of applications; for example, the data backend for web or mobile applications.

For the rest of this chapter, we dig further into these project types by focusing on the following for each project type:

Primary considerations

Although these three project types share many commonalities, there will also be distinctions that will affect architectural decisions and priorities. These decisions in turn will drive the rest of the project. When looking at our three project types, we begin by detailing these primary considerations for the particular project type.

Risk management

Any data project brings with it a set of risks. We discuss possible risks associated with the project type and how to deal with these risks. In many cases, there will be multiple approaches to risk management based on specific use cases, so we need to explore this aspect along different dimensions.

 We cover risk management in more detail in Chapter 3.

Team makeup

There are considerations regarding staffing teams to deliver the different project types. The types of skills, experience, and interests will vary with the different project types, so we provide some recommendations around building successful teams for each project type.

Security

Another important consideration that will likely apply to all of your projects is security. This is an extensive and important topic that deserves its own book; in fact, there are useful references depending on which systems you're using. Because this is such an important topic, we won't go into detail in this book, but it's useful to enumerate the security concerns that you should keep in mind throughout your projects.

It's worth noting that security was more of an afterthought for some open source data management systems. This was because early users were more concerned with technical considerations related to the ability to store and process large volumes of data. Additionally, these systems were generally deployed on internal networks with controlled access. As enterprises began deploying these solutions, concerns about security and sensitivity of the data being stored in these systems became paramount, leading to projects and vendors working on changes and enhancements to harden these systems for enterprise use.

The following are the different dimensions that you should be considering when planning for security in your projects:

Authentication
> Ensuring that users accessing the system are who they claim to be. Any mature system should offer support for strong authentication, typically through an authentication protocol like Kerberos or Lightweight Directory Access Protocol (LDAP).

Authorization
> After you've ensured that a valid user is accessing a system, you need to determine which data they're allowed to access. A mature system will offer the ability to control access at different levels of granularity; for example, not just at a database table level, but down to column-level access. Having control over which users and groups are able to access specific data is important when building a data architecture for which the security of data is critical.

Encryption
> In addition to controlling access to data, when security is a concern, it's also important to protect that data from malicious users and intrusions. Encryption of data is a common way to help achieve this. We need to consider this from two different angles:
>
> - *Data at rest*. This is data that has landed in your system and is stored on disk. Many data management vendors offer solutions as part of their platform for managing this, and several third-party vendors offer solutions.
>
> - *Data on the wire*. This is the data that's moving through your system. Generally, vendors or projects will support this via standard encryption mechanisms such as Transport Layer Security (TLS).

Auditing
> The final dimension to security is being able to capture activity related to data in your system, including the lineage of the data, who and what is accessing the data, how it's being used, and so on. Here again, look for tools that are provided by a vendor or project to help address this.

If security is important to your use cases, the best approach will be to look for solutions or vendors that can address these four areas. This will allow you to spend more time focusing on solving your problems and less time on the details of managing the security of your data.

Data Pipelines and Data Staging

We begin our discussion with the data project type that has the widest scope of the three because it involves the path of data from external data sources to destination data sources and will provide the basis for building out the rest of your data use cases.

In this particular case, we need to design our solution with the following in mind:

- Types of queries, processing, and so on that we'll be performing against the destination data
- Any customer-facing data requirements
- Types of data collected in terms of its value

Because of the importance of this data in implementing further analysis and processing, it's crucial that we pay careful attention to modeling and storing the data in a way that facilitates further access.

Primary Considerations and Risk Management

We can break this use case into a number of primary considerations, which we discuss further in the subsequent sections:

- Consumption of source data
- Guarantees around data delivery
- Data governance
- Latency and confirmations of delivery
- Access patterns against the destination data

Let's look at these considerations and how attributes of each will affect our priorities.

Source data consumption

When we talk about data sources, we're basically talking about the things that create the data that's required for building your solutions. Sources could be anything from phones, sensors, applications, machine logs, operational and transactional databases, and so on. The source itself is mostly out of scope of your pipeline and staging use cases. In fact, you can evaluate the success of your scoping by how much of your time you spend working with the source team. The more time your data engineering team spends on source integration can often be inversely correlated to how well designed the source integration is.

There are standard approaches we can use for source data collection:

Embedded code
> This is when you provide code embedded within the source system that knows how to send required data into your data pipeline.

Agents
> This is an independent system that is close to the source and in many cases is on the same device. This is different from the embedded code example because the agents run as separate processes with no dependency concerns.

Interfaces
> This is the lightest of the options. An example would be a Representational State Transfer (REST) or WebSocket endpoint that receives data sent by the sources.

It should be noted that there are other commonly used options to perform data collection; for example:

- Third-party data integration tools, either open source or commercial
- Batch data ingest tools such as Apache Sqoop or tools provided with specific projects; for example, the Hadoop Distributed File System (HDFS) put command

Depending on your use case, these options can be useful in building your pipelines and worth considering. Because they're already covered in other references or vendor and project documentation, we don't cover these options further in this section.

Which approach is best is often determined by the sources of data, but in some cases multiple approaches might be suitable. The more important part can be ensuring a correct implementation, so let's discuss some considerations around these different collection types, starting with the embedded code option.

Embedded code. Consider the following guidelines when implementing embedded code as part of source data collection:

Limit implementation languages
> Don't try to support multiple programming languages; instead, implement with a single language and then use bindings for other languages. For example, consider using C, C++, or Java and then create bindings for other languages that you need to support. As an example of this, consider Kafka, which includes a Java producer and consumer as part of the core project, whereas other libraries or clients for other languages require binding to libraries that are included as part of the Kafka distribution.

Limit dependencies

A problem with any embedded piece of code is potential library conflicts. Making efforts to limit dependencies can help mitigate this issue.

Provide visibility

With any embedded code, there can be concerns with what is under the hood. Providing access to code—for example, by open sourcing the code or at least providing the code via a public repository—provides an easy and safe way to relieve these fears. The user can then get full view of the code to alleviate potential concerns involving things like memory usage, network usage, and so on.

Operationalizing code

Another consideration is possible production issues with embedded code. Make sure you've taken into account things like memory leaks or performance issues and have defined a support model. Logging and instrumentation of code can help to ensure that you have the ability to debug issues when they arise.

Version management

When code is embedded, you likely won't be able to control the scheduling of things like updates. Ensuring things like backward compatibility and well-defined versions is key.

Agents. The following are things to keep in mind when using agents in your architecture:

Deployment

As with other components in your architecture, make sure deployment of agents is tested and repeatable. This might mean using some type of automation tool or containers.

Resource usage

Ensure that the source systems have sufficient resources to reliably support the agent processes, including memory, CPU, and so on.

Isolation

Even through agents run externally from the processing applications, you'll still want to protect against problems with the agent that can negatively affect data collection.

Debugging

Again, here we want to take steps to ensure that we can debug and recover from inevitable production issues. This might mean logging, instrumentation, and so forth.

Interfaces. Following are some guidelines for using interfaces:

Versioning

Versioning again is an issue here, although less painful than the embedded solution. Just make sure your interface has versioning as a core concept from day one.

Performance

With any source collection framework, performance and throughput are critical. Additionally, even if you design and implement code to ensure performance, you might find that source or sink implementations are suboptimal. Because you might not control this code, having a way to detect and notify when performance issues surface will be important.

Security

While in the agent and embedded models you control the code that is talking to you, in the interface model you have only the interface as a barrier to entry. The key is to keep the interface simple while still injecting security. There are a number of models for this such as using security tokens.

Risk management for data consumption

The risks that you need to worry about when building out a data source collection system include everything you would normally worry about for an externally facing API as well as concerns related to scale. Let's look at some of the major concerns that you need to be looking for.

Version management. Everyone loves a good API that just works. The problem is that we rarely can design interfaces with such foresight that they won't require incompatible changes at some point. You will want to have a robust versioning strategy and a plan for providing backward compatibility guarantees to protect against this as well as ensuring that this plan is part of your communication strategy.

Impacts from source failures. There are a number of possible failure scenarios at the source layer for which you need to plan. For example, if you have embedded code that's part of the source execution process, a failure in your code can lead to an overall failure in data collection. Additionally, even if you don't have embedded code, if there's a failure in your collection mechanism such as an agent, how is the source affected? Is there data loss? Can this affect expected uptime for the application?

The answer to this is to have options and know your sources and communicate those different options with clear understanding that failure and downtime will happen. This will allow adding any required safeguards to protect against these possible failure scenarios.

Note that failure in the data pipeline should be a rare occurrence for a well-designed and implemented pipeline, but it will inevitably happen. Because failure is inevitable, our pipelines need to have mechanisms in place to alert us when undesired things take place. Examples would be monitoring of things like throughput and alerting when metrics are seen to deviate from specific thresholds. The idea is to build the most resilient pipelines for the use case but have insight into when things go wrong.

Additionally, consider having replicated pipelines. In failure cases, if one pipeline goes down, another can take over. This is more than node failure protection; having a separate pipeline protects you from difficult-to-predict failures like badly configured deployments or a bad build getting pushed. Ideally, we should design our pipelines in a way that we can deploy them as simply as you would deploy a web application.

Protection from sources that behave poorly.   When you build a data ingestion system, it's possible that sources might misuse your APIs, send too much data, and so on. Any of these actions could have negative effects on your system. As you design and implement your system, make sure to put in place mechanisms to protect against these risks. These might include considerations like the following:

Throttling
> This will limit the number of records a source can send you. As the source sends you more records, your system can increase the time to accept that data. Additionally, you might even need to send a message indicating that the source is making too many connections.

Dropping
> If your system doesn't provide guarantees, you could simply drop messages if you become overloaded or have trouble processing input data. However, opening the door to this can introduce a belief that your system is lossy and can lower the overall trust in your system. Under most circumstances, though, being lossy might be fine as long as it is communicated to the source that loss is happening in real time so that clients can take appropriate action. In short, whenever pursuing the approach of dropping data, make sure your clients have full knowledge of when and why.

Data delivery guarantees

When planning a data pipeline, there are a number of promises that you will need to give to the owners of the data you're collecting. With any data collection system, you can offer different levels of guarantees:

Best effort
> If a message is sent to you, you try to deliver it, but data loss is possible. This is suitable when you're not concerned with capturing every event. An example

might be if you're performing processing on incoming data to capture aggregate metrics for which total precision isn't required.

At least once

If a message is sent to you, you might duplicate it, but you won't lose it. This will probably be the most common use case. Although it adds some complexity over best effort, in most cases you'll probably want to ensure that all events are captured in your pipeline. Note that this might also require adding logic in your pipeline to deduplicate data, but in most cases this is probably easier and less expensive to implement than the exactly-once option described next.

Exactly once

If a message is received by the pipeline, you guarantee that it's processed and will never be duplicated. As we noted, this is the most expensive and technically complex option. Although many systems now promise to provide this, you should carefully consider whether this is necessary or whether you can put other mechanisms in place to account for potential duplicate records.

Again, for most use cases at least once is likely suitable given that it's often less expensive to perform deduplication after ingesting data. Regardless of the level of guarantee, you should plan for, document, and communicate this to users of the system.

Data management and governance

A robust data collection system today must have two critical features:

Data model management

This is the ability to change or add data models.

Data regulation

This is the ability to know everything that is being collected and the risks that might exist if that data is misused or exposed.

 We talk more about this when we cover metadata management in Chapter 6, but for now let's look at them in terms of scope and goals.

Data model management. You need to have mechanisms in place to capture your system's data models, and, ideally, this should mean that groups using your data pipeline don't need to engage your team to make a new data feed or change an existing data feed. An example of a system that provides an approach for this is the Confluent Schema Registry for Kafka, which allows for the storage of schemas, including multiple versions of schemas. This provides support for backward compatibility for different versions of applications that access data in the system.

Declaring a schema is only part of the problem. You might also need the following mechanisms:

Registration
> The definition of a new data feed along with its schema.

Routing
> Which data feeds should go to which topics, processing systems, and possible storage systems.

Sampling
> An extension to routing, with the added feature of removing part of the data. This is ideal for a staging environment and for testing.

Access controls
> Who will be able to see the data, both in final persisted state and off the stream.

Metadata captured
> The ability to attach metadata to fields.

Additional features that you will find in more advanced systems include the following:

Transformational logic
> The ability to transform the data in custom ways before it lands in the staging areas.

Aggregation and sessionization
> Transformational logic that understands how to perform operations on data windows.

Regulatory concerns. As more data is collected, stored, and analyzed, concern for things like data protection and privacy have grown. This, of course, means that you need to have plans in place to respond to regulations as well as protecting against external hacks, internal misuse, and so on. Part of this is making sure that you have a clear understanding and catalog of all the data you collect; we return to this topic in Chapter 6.

Latency and delivery confirmation

Unlike the requirements of a real-time system, a data pipeline normally gets a lot of leeway when it comes to latency and confirmations of delivery. However, this is a very important area for you to scope and define expectations. Let's define these two terms and what you'll need to establish with respect to each.

Latency. This is the time it takes from when a source publishes information until that information is accessible by a given processing layer or a given staging system. To illustrate this, we use the example of a stream-processing application. For this example, assume that we have data coming in through Kafka that is being consumed by a Flink or Spark Streaming application. That application might then be sending alerts based on the outcome of processing to downstream systems. In this case, we can quantify latency into multiple buckets, as illustrated in Figure 1-1.

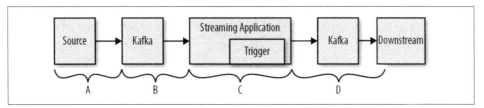

Figure 1-1. Quantifying system latency

Let's take a closer look at each bucket:

- **A**: Time to get from the source to Kafka. This can be a direct shot, in which case we are talking about the time to buffer and send over the network. However, there might be a fan-in architecture that includes load balancers, microservices, or other hops that can result in increased latency.

- **B**: Time to get through Kafka will depend on a number of things such as the Kafka configuration and consumer configuration.

- **C**: Time between when the processing engine receives the event to when it triggers on the event. With some engines like Spark Streaming, triggering happens on a time interval, whereas others like Flink can have lower latency. This will also be affected by configuration as well as use cases.

- **D**: Again, we have the time to get into Kafka and be read from Kafka. Latency here will be highly dependent on buffering and polling configurations in the producer and consumer.

Delivery confirmation. With respect to a data pipeline, delivery confirmations let the source know when the data has arrived at different stages in your pipeline and could even let the source know if the data has reached the staging area. Here are some guidelines on designing this into your system:

Do you really need confirmation?
> The advantage of confirmation is that it allows the source to resend data in the event of a failure; for example, a network issue or hardware failure. Because failure is inevitable, providing confirmation will likely be suitable for most use cases.

However, if this is not a requirement, you can reduce the time and complexity to implement your pipeline, so make sure to confirm whether you really need confirmation.

How to deliver the confirmation?
If you do need to provide confirmations, you need to add this to your design. This will likely include selecting software solutions that provide confirmation functionality and building logic into any custom code you implement as part of your pipeline. Because there's some complexity involved in providing delivery confirmation, as much as possible try to use existing solutions that can provide this.

Risk management for data delivery

Data delivery promises can be risky. For one, you want to be able to offer a system that gives users everything they want, but in the real world, things can and will go awry, and at some point, your guarantees might fail.

There are two suggested ways to deal with this risk. The first is to have a clean architecture that's shared with stakeholders in order to solicit input that might help to ensure stability. Additionally, having adequate metrics and logging is important to validate that the implementation has met the requirements.

Additionally, you will want a mechanism that will notify users and the source systems when guarantees are being missed. This will provide time to adjust or switch to a backup system seamlessly.

Access patterns

The last focus of the data pipeline use case is access patterns for the data. What's important to call out here are the types of access and requirements that you should plan for when defining your data pipeline.

We can break this into two groupings: access to data, and retention of data. Let's look at data access and the types of jobs that will most likely come up as priorities. This includes the following:

- Batch jobs that do large scans and aggregations
- Streaming jobs that do large scans
- Point data requests; for example, random access
- Search queries

Batch jobs with large scans. Batch jobs that scan large blocks of data are core workloads of data research and analytics. Let's run through four typical workload types that fit into this categorization to help with defining this category. To gain a solid grasp on the concept, let's discuss some real-world use cases with respect to a supermarket chain:

Analytical SQL

> This might entail using SQL to do rollups of which items are selling by zip code and date. It would be very common that reports like this would run daily and be visible to leadership within the company.

Sessionization

> Using SQL or tools like Apache Spark, we might want to *sessionize* the buying habits of our customers; for example, to better predict their individual shopping needs and patterns and be alerted to churn risks.

Model training

> A possible use case for machine learning in our supermarket example is a recommendation solution that would look at the shopping habits of our customers and provide suggestions for items based on customers' known preferences.

Scenario predictions evaluation

> In the supermarket use case, we need to define a strategy for deciding how to order the items to fill shelves in our stores. We can use historical data to know whether our purchasing model is effective.

The important point here is that we want the data for long periods of time, and we want to be able to bring a large amount of processing power to our analytics in order to produce actionable outcomes.

Streaming jobs with large scans. There are two main differences between batch and streaming workloads: the time between execution of the job, and the idea of progressive workloads. With respect to time, streaming jobs are normally thought to be in the range of millisecond to minutes, whereas batch workloads are generally minutes to hours or even days. The progressive workload is maybe the bigger difference because it is a difference in the output of the job. Let's look at our four types of jobs and see how progressiveness affects them:

Analytical SQL

> With streaming jobs, our rollups and reports will update at smaller intervals like seconds or minutes, allowing for visibility into near-real-time changes for faster reaction time. Additionally, ideally the processing expense will not be that much bigger than batch because we are working on only the newly added data and not reprocessing past data.

Sessionization

> As with the rollups, sessionization in streaming jobs also happens in smaller intervals, allowing more real-time actionable results. Consider that in our supermarket example we use sessionization to analyze the items our customers put

into their cart and, by doing so, predict what they plan to make for dinner. With that knowledge, we might also be able to suggest items for dessert that are new to the customer.

Model training

Not all models lend themselves to real-time training. However, the trained models might be ideal for real-time execution to make real-time actionable calls in our business.

Scenario predictions evaluation

Additionally, now that we are making real-time calls with technology, we need a real-time way to evaluate those decisions to power humans to know whether corrections need to be made. As we move to more automation in terms of decision making, we need to match that with real-time evaluation.

Where the batch processing needs massive storage and massive compute, the streaming component really only needs enough compute, storage, and memory to hold windows in context.

 We talk more about stream processing in Chapter 8.

Point requests.   Until now, we have talked about access patterns that are looking at all of the data either in given tables or partitions, or through a stream. The idea with point requests is that we want to fetch a specific record or data point very fast and with high concurrency.

Think about the following use cases for our supermarket example:

- Look up the current items in stock for a given store
- Look up the current location of items being shipped to your store
- Look up the complete supply chain for items in your store
- Look up events over time and be able to scan forward and backward in time to investigate how those events affect things like sales

When we explore storage in Chapter 5, we'll go through indexable storage solutions that will be optimal for these use cases. For now, just be aware that this category is about items or events in time related to an entity and being able to fetch that information in real time at scale.

Searchable access. The last access pattern that is very common is searchable access to data. In this use case, access patterns need to be fast while also allowing for flexibility in queries. Thinking about our supermarket use case, you might want to quickly learn what types of vegetables are in stock, or maybe look at all shipments from a specific farm because there was a contamination.

 We talk more about solutions to target these use cases when we examine storage in Chapter 5.

Risk management for access patterns

In previous sections, the focus was on data sources and creating data pipelines to make the data available in a system. In this section, we talk about making data available to people who want to use it, which means a completely different group of stakeholders. Another consideration is that access pattern requirements might change more rapidly simply because of the larger user base trying to extract value from the data. This is why we've organized our discussion of access patterns into four key offerings. If you can find a small set of core access patterns and make them work at scale, you can extend them for many use cases.

With that being said, doing the following will help ensure that you manage risks associated with access patterns:

- Help ensure that users are using the right access patterns for their use case.
- Make sure your storage systems are available and resilient.
- Verify that your offering is meeting your users' needs. If they are copying your data into another system to do work, that could be a sign that your offering is not good enough.

Pipeline and Staging Team Makeup

Now that we have walked through primary considerations and risks for pipeline and staging use cases, you might have begun to get an idea of the types of people that you want on these teams. The following are some job roles to consider:

Service and support engineers
These are engineers who are tasked with working with users, including stakeholders of source data systems, users accessing data in the system, and so on. These engineers are trained to do the following:

- Optimally use the system
- Look for good use cases for users of the system
- Work with the team to address issues being faced by users
- Advocate for users
- Help users be successful

System engineers/administrators

These are engineers who are obsessed with uptime, latency, efficiency, failure, and data integrity. They don't need to care much for the real use cases for the system; rather, they focus more on the reliability of the system and its performance.

Data engineers

These are engineers who know the data and the types of storage systems within your system. Their main job is to make sure that the data offerings are being used correctly and that the appropriate big data solutions are being used for the right thing. These are experts in data storage and data processing.

Data architects

These are experts in data modeling who can define the structures that can define how data in the system should be structured. In some cases, this role might be assumed by the data engineers on the team.

Data Processing and Analysis

These are the projects for which we use the data populated by the data pipeline and staging projects and then transform and analyze the data to derive value. We've already talked a little about transformation and value creation in the previous discussion. However, that discussion mainly focused on preparing the data for use in our data processing and analysis applications. In this section, we examine the use cases that perform those transformations and analysis on the data to derive value.

Primary Considerations and Risk Management

We focus on the following high-level items when we're evaluating this type of use case:

- Defining the problems that we're trying to solve
- Implementing and operationalizing the processing and analysis to solve the problems we've identified

In short, what do we want to do, how do we get there, how do we make it repeatable, and how do we quantify its value when we get there?

Defining the problems to be solved

In many cases, your business will already know many of the questions that need to be answered to provide value. Often, though, determining the appropriate questions to ask and which are the correct problems to solve for your business can be a challenge. This is especially true when there are many possible questions to pursue, some of which are potentially impactful, others cool and interesting. Other times the questions we should be asking aren't even obvious.

So, the first focus here is really not about the data or what we want to do with the data, but about the value we want to derive from the data; what will make an impact to our business, and what can be actionable? Determining the answers to these questions requires talking to stakeholders—the users and customers of your systems. Often, the challenges here can be getting the time and attention of these stakeholders and, unfortunately, it's often the case that even they won't know what they really need.

The following are some good questions to ask yourself and users during this process:

- What are the most important things to capture in terms of trackable metrics?
- What are things that affect customer engagement?
- Is there a gap in the company's offerings?
- Are there active pain points?

A good next step is to try to further define our objectives in solving the problem. This will generally mean defining specific metrics, numbers, visualizations, and so on that we can use to help evaluate approaches to solving the problem and determine whether and how other potential issues might relate to the problem we're addressing.

Let's take this idea and apply it to our supermarket example. Suppose that our problem is a concern that shelves are not fully stocked with the proper products. We could create visualizations to help illustrate this, such as the following:

Products stocked over time
A time-based chart that shows the average, max, min, top 10%, and bottom 10% of inventory for each product

Products out of stock
A time-based chart illustrating times when each item is unstocked

These charts will help us drill into additional visualizations that can help us define the impact of this problem; for example:

Substitute purchase patterns
During times when a product is out of stock, do customers select a different product?

Delivery supply chain

For products that are understocked, was the problem caused by delivery delays?

Region or store variations

Are there differences in stock levels across regions or stores?

Customer impact

For customers who are normal purchasers of the understocked items, do we see a change in spending between time periods when inventory levels are acceptable and when the item is out of stock?

The idea is to provide context that will help illustrate the problem, provide scope around the problem, and show potential impact of the problem. It's possible that this exercise will provide enough information to drive actionable decisions. This information will also play a role in determining how important this problem is to solve versus other problems facing the company.

Risk management for problem definition

When identifying problems that need to be solved, two important considerations can help you manage risk and will affect further efforts:

Get many viewpoints

Make sure that you get input from multiple sources, not just one or two. Examples would be just talking to top management or a team directly affected by the problem. The issue is that different groups might be too close or too far from the problem to be able to see it from all angles. Having the additional perspectives can help you in terms of how to later quantify and solve the problem.

Build trust

You want to be seen as a collaborator, and not somebody trying to find shortcomings or issues within the organization. Be sure that you work closely with stakeholders to gain trust.

The challenge at this stage is confirming that you're defining the correct problem and capturing it correctly. An effective way to address this concern is to communicate about the problem you're trying to solve often and openly. This might seem like common sense but can often help avoid the perception of placing blame or responsibility on parts of the organization. It can sometimes be the case that putting the focus on a specific problem can have the appearance of putting people or groups in your organization in a negative light.

The way around these political traps can be to find cross-departmental contacts that understand the iterative process of problem definition and then communicating often with these folks to reduce any nasty surprises.

Implementing and operationalizing solutions

Now that we have a handle on the problem and we've explored solutions, we're ready to move on to implementing these solutions. While keeping in mind the original problem we're trying solve, it's important to remain flexible and adapt to new information that might affect our solution.

A couple of important considerations to be mindful of during the implementation phase are to focus on building the right components in a robust way to ensure that you're not just creating one-off solutions, and to operationalize solutions.

Building a robust solution. A common trap is to build out systems that solve a single problem. A better approach is to build systems that can provide a platform for solving multiple problems. Being able to get results quickly and correctly is good, but even better is to be able to find all (or as many as possible) of the answers quickly and correctly. → build ingestion patterns, not pipelines

You want to ensure that you define a clear path to value. A useful way of doing this can be to create a block diagram, such as that depicted in Figure 1-2, that goes from top to bottom to help visualize your path. On the uppermost side you put all the data sources, and as you move from top to the bottom, you get closer and closer to value and actionable products.

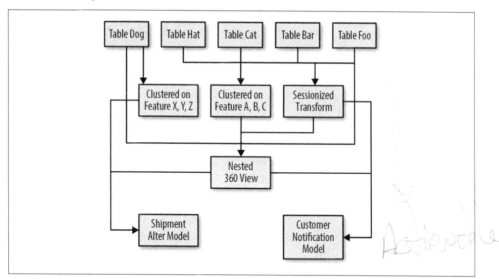

Figure 1-2. Breaking a system into blocks

Think of this as building blocks. You want to build blocks like the Nested 360 view that can be useful for addressing many problems; not just the current ones, but also future needs.

The risk to building too many blocks that have single uses is that every block must be maintained. At some point, there can be value in consolidating blocks; the goal should be to streamline your paths to value.

On the other hand, if you try to build a system to solve every problem, you might end up with a system that's not well suited to solve any problem. It's always good to start small and make sure you have a clear understanding of the business requirements.

Operationalizing solutions.   A common trap is trusting the same people who find the problems or solve the problems to operationalize the solutions, because these different activities require completely different skill sets. You will want a good pipeline and communication between these two groups. It's also important that you make the same commitment to operationalizing solutions as to actually finding the solutions.

Data Processing and Analytics Team Makeup

Unlike the pipeline and staging team, teams that can successfully use data to provide value need to be more focused on problem discovery, working across teams, and finding paths to solutions. This means that we need a different mix of people:

Problem seekers
> These are people who are able to earn trust with different groups in your company and are adept at identifying and quantifying problems. Think of them as treasure hunters who need to build alliances and search through the weeds of everyday business to find problems to solve that will have a high impact. These folks could have different roles within your team such as project managers, product managers, and technical leads, but could also be the individual developers and analysts on a team.

Architects
> A requirement for a successful problem-solving group is to pick not only the right problems to solve, but also the correct order. This applies very much to the block building idea; we want to pick the problems to build with the least effort and that include reusable parts.

The brains
> These are the data scientists and analysts who will help come up with solutions.

The engineers
> You'll need a group of engineers who know how to work with all of the aforementioned parties and how to take their work and productionize it.

Solution communication experts
> As we just mentioned, finding a solution can be perceived as pointing fingers. Additionally, a solution with no buy-in will never see real-life implementation. It

is these communication experts who are able to evangelize the solutions so that they get to reach their full potential. This will probably be the project managers, product managers, or technical leads on a project.

Application Development

So, up until this point, we have talked about data pipelines that land data in staging areas, then we talked about projects focused on exploring data and gaining value from that data. Whereas those two use case categories are more about data gathering and learning, this final use case category is about deploying applications that use our data to provide some service to users, either internal or external. A good example of this might be a website that relies on the data to drive functionality. The assumption here is that the data is being used to drive applications that support large numbers of users, requiring scalability, reliability, and availability.

Primary Considerations and Risk Management

In this use case, key considerations to help ensure success include the following:

Latency and throughput
> How long does it take to execute an operation, and how many operations can the system handle per second?

State locality and consistency
> If your system is available in more than one region, how is replication handled? Is it siloed, eventually replicated, or strongly locked?

Availability of systems
> What are the failure and recovery characteristics of the system?

Latency and throughput

When building out requirements for an application, a good place to begin is learning what data you need to have saved and how you're going to interact with that data. For example, this interaction might be number of operations: inserts, updates, multiple-row transactions, and so on.

There are number of potential concerns we need to be considering for every data interaction in our design:

Race conditions. For example, if two clients update the same row at the same time, who wins? There are ways to address this, with the following being a few examples:

Last one wins
> In this design, it doesn't matter, and they just randomly overwrite each other.

Transactional locking
> This mean that there is a lock either at a data-store level or the server level before mutation is allowed. A common example is making a mutation only if another condition is true; for example, updating column foo to 42 if column bar equals 100.

Asynchronous versus synchronous operations. In systems that require very low latency, it might be unrealistic to save in real time. There might be a desire to have state in server or client memory and persist to the final store asynchronously. When looking at the use case requirements for this, you need to consider the following:

Speed versus truth
> With an asynchronous model, there is a short window during which there is a chance for data loss. You need to evaluate how important that is compared to latency.

Performance consistency. Does the tested performance hold? There are many questions to be asked here:

- What if the insertion order changes?
- Will the performance change as the data scales?
- Does performance change as the storage solution grows?
- If there a difference between generated data and real data?
- How will performance be affected by maintenance work?

Risk management for latency

The best way to mitigate risk in relation to performance is to test early and often and communicate always. Everything around performance should be monitored like crazy. You need to fully document every connection, be it internal or external. Additionally, you should question results often. Have more than one team test the results.

Lastly, make sure you use interfaces in your design—as we discuss in Chapter 4—so that you can swap out implementations for other implementations. The odds are high that you will think of a better strategy after you build the first solution. Give yourself some room to implement those changes without having to rewrite your entire system.

State locality. There are a number of places where state can exist. In a distributed system, we can highlight four major locations to hold state:

Clients
> The client-side interface the user is using

Server
> The server or servers that the client accesses

Datacenter
> Persistence with the local datacenter housing the application servers

Multidatacenter
> Replicated persistence across datacenters

When looking at use case goals and requirements, there are things to consider for each of these scenarios.

Client. Caching data in the client and allowing client-side mutation provides high performance and scalability. However, there a couple potential problems with client-side state:

Ephemeral
> The client can die at any time, causing data loss before data reaches the server.

Trust
> The client runs on potentially untrusted hosts, with untrusted users, which can cause issues where client trust is important.

Server. Although on the server side we should not be concerned with trust issues, there can still be concern with ephemeral data being lost. Another potential concern with the server is user partitioning. Whereas a client is probably partitioned one per user, a server is partitioned by groups of users. In some cases, user partitioning is based on a clear strategy; for example, with a game application that needs to maintain user state within a single server. In many cases, though, user placement is more random; for example, a web application for which user placement is based on a load balancer.

In use cases that might require multiserver state management, we might need to consider datacenter persistence.

Datacenter. This layer is where you'd see state persistence for common technologies like NoSQL systems, relational databases, and distributed caches. The goal with this layer is to store all the state needed for this local region and the server and clients within this region.

The data in this datacenter will most likely be replicated and protected from failure of one or more nodes, although that doesn't mean it is perfectly protected. It's not unheard of for regions to go down. If this is a concern in your use case, this is where a multidatacenter approach might be required.

Multidatacenter. There are several models for the multidatacenter scenario; which ones you use will depend on the requirements for your use case. Let's look at a couple that might apply to you:

Replication for disaster recovery
> In this example, we use a multidatacenter configuration to provide protection against data loss, for example, if an entire datacenter becomes unavailable. This is normally an asynchronous or batch process in which data becomes eventually consistent across datacenters. We're not looking for completely consistent state locally, but only that it is moving in that direction. This won't protect against all data loss, but it does protect against most of it.
>
> A concern with using replication alone is what happens if items are being mutated in multiple regions at the same time? We don't have globally consistent state, so there's no single source of truth.

Locking
> Global locking is one solution to ensuring consistency across regions in cases of mutated data. The idea here is a resource is globally locked to a region. No one can mutate that resource until they get the lock. There are a number of designs to support this:
>
> *Locking mutation to a client*
>> Every client will need to obtain a lock to change the given record.
>
> *Locking mutation to a datacenter*
>> All mutations have to go through a given datacenter first. This requires less locking than the client scenario but will result in higher network latencies for clients that happen to be outside the region.
>
> *Locking at the record level*
>> This is essentially a quorum architecture in which we have an odd number of locations storing state, and as long as a majority agree with the state, the changes are accepted.

A factor to keep in mind is that generally the data within a datacenter is limited to the users within the given region. If your application requires interaction between clients in different regions, you need to think about how different regions will share their data.

Risk management for locality

It's important to have a strategy about state early in your project planning; what are the requirements and goals of your project? How do decisions about state affect the user? These are difficult things to change after a project is underway.

After you have made your decision, you should fully document these choices and all effects on the user need to be enumerated. This documentation needs to be in a format that's accessible to all users and that clearly communicates the impact.

Availability

Availability of systems is of course a critical concern, but also challenging. Multiple things can affect the uptime of your systems, including the following:

Human errors
　　People make mistakes; a bad configuration change, a deployment of a wrong version of code, and so on.

Upgrades
　　Some upgrades will require the system to be restarted. Even in the case of rolling restarts, there are parts of the system that need to be unavailable for some period.

Failures
　　Hardware failures are inevitable, regardless of whether you're running systems on-premises or in the cloud.

Attacks
　　Malicious attacks are also something for which you must plan, given that they have the potential to affect the availability of your systems.

You'll need to be able to define the failure and recovery scenarios that are acceptable for your given service-level agreements (SLAs). Here are some examples of failure points and recovery plans:

Server failover
　　In the case of an active server failing, you need to be able to failover to another server. If your state is at the datacenter, a single server failure should have little or no impact.

Nonreplicated cache failover
　　There are some designs for which a cache is populated with a partition of the state needed to support your use case. When that cache is destroyed because of a failure, the data might be persistent in other stores; however, it takes time to restore that cache.

Eventually replicated datacenter failover
　　A common way to do replication over a wide-area network is eventual replication. In case of failure, requests can switch to different datacenters and continue operating. However, there are two main problems with multidatacenter failover: first, you have a strong chance of losing data that is about to be in flight; this window will hopefully be small and it will depend on your throughput and your latency. The second problem is determining how to manage writes; for example,

choosing between having a leader that manages writes or just accepting writes to any datacenter.

Risk management for availability

A good strategy to address potential scenarios that can affect your availability is to intentionally introduce failure into your system on a regular basis; for example, using a tool like Chaos Monkey (*https://github.com/Netflix/chaosmonkey*), developed by Netflix.

The results of these failure tests should be used to define the impact, recovery plans, and steps to make the failure less impactful in the future. Publishing this as part of the system is not a bad idea and will provide users of the system a better window into real expectations.

Additionally, if you do this properly, you can develop a culture that not only is thinking failure first but is motivated to reduce the impacts of failure.

Application Development Team Makeup

Unlike our other two use cases, application development is about direct user impact, consistency, behavior, and efficiency of data movement. Although you might have some of the same resources you had on the pipeline use case, there are some notable differences. Specifically, consider the following types of resources as part of your application development team:

Site reliability engineers (SREs)
These are engineers who are dedicated to ensuring the reliability and scalability of applications deployed to production. These resources will be critical to the success of the deployment of your applications.

Database engineers
These probably won't be traditional database developers and architects, but rather people who have a deep understanding of modern distributed data storage and processing systems. These are the folks who are going to make sure that reading, writing, and transactions are executing at the high and consistent speed you need to make your product viable.

Summary

This has been a long chapter with a lot of material, but it's important that you have a good understanding of your projects and go through a thorough planning process before moving forward with implementation. To facilitate this process, we've broken data projects into the three most common categories:

Data pipelines and staging
> These are projects that involve bringing source data into your systems and pre-paring them for further processing. These projects will provide the basis for all other types of projects in your organization, so it's critically important to pay careful attention when planning these projects.

Data processing and analysis
> After the data is available, these are projects that seek to gain actionable insights from your data by performing processing and analysis of the data. These projects might be ad hoc explorations performed by analysts or full-blown projects that drive reports and dashboards for business users.

Applications
> These are user-facing applications that provide services and value to users, either internal or external. These projects will generally rely on successful implementations and deployments of the previous two project types.

For each of these project types, we discussed considerations that should drive your project planning and development. We broke these considerations into three types:

Primary considerations
> Unique considerations that you should include in your planning for each project type

Risk
> Likely project risks for which you should plan, and information to help you mitigate these risks

Project teams
> Roles that you should consider when forming teams to deliver each project type

The guidelines in this chapter are based on our experience working on multiple projects across different companies. They should help to ensure the success of your data projects. We'll also cover some of these topics in more detail in the next chapters.

CHAPTER 2

Evaluating and Selecting Data Management Solutions

You're likely already aware of the importance of technology selection when embarking on a new project. Choosing the correct solutions is a complex process that will have long-lasting impacts on your organization and a direct impact to the success (or failure) of your data projects. Do you reuse trusted solutions, do you try something new, or do you follow examples of leaders in the industry? There are difficult decisions we must face when selecting solutions.

As you move through this decision-making process, you'll likely be presented with market hype, extravagant promises from vendors, analysts with varied agendas, and tools with enthusiastic user bases. Some of these solutions might be good fits for your projects, whereas others will be poor fits that lead to wasted time, money, and frustration.

The goal of this chapter is to help guide you to the best choices as you move through the technology selection process. We begin by discussing some common life cycles of open source projects; this knowledge will help in understanding how healthy a project is, where it is in the life cycle, and whether it's a potential fit regardless of the hype that might or might not accompany the project. Then, we talk about how to evaluate claims, such as the results of performance or benchmark testing. Lastly, we dig into different patterns for picking the right technologies for your projects.

A natural question to ask is: why focus on open source projects in this chapter? What about commercial solutions? A major reason is that many of the newer big data platforms are open source projects, and even many modern proprietary solutions are built on or utilize open source software, or in some cases attempt to replicate the functionality of an open source solution. There are of course exceptions to this— Teradata is a good example of commercial closed-source data management software that can store and process big data. In the cloud space, Amazon Web Services (AWS) offers proprietary offerings such as Simple Storage Service (Amazon S3) or Kinesis that are designed to manage big data storage and processing. Even in these propriet-ary software cases, though, the product development will often follow a similar path as open source projects but, of course, hidden from public view. Where it is relevant throughout the chapter, we outline differences between open and closed-source offerings.

This focus on open source projects is not intended to suggest that commercial third-party solutions don't have a place in your data projects. Most enterprise software ven-dors are supporting the major big data platforms and can often provide solutions that will facilitate your application development, particularly if you're already using the solution elsewhere in your organization. Also note that many of the decision points that relate to open source projects will be applicable to commercial offerings, as well.

It's also important to note that many software vendors are embracing a hybrid propri-etary and open source model. Going back to the example of Teradata, although its flagship offerings are proprietary, the company has also embraced open source soft-ware; for example, in its support for Apache Presto as well as other open source sys-tems. Another example is AWS, which in addition to providing proprietary services, also provides services built on open source software such as Apache Hadoop.

Another thing to note as you read through this chapter is that most of the considera-tions here apply more to software that you're deploying and managing, either on-premises or in the cloud. This is in contrast to managed services provided by cloud or managed service provider vendors. Although many of the considerations discussed here and elsewhere in the book will also be useful in selecting managed service offer-ings, to a large extent your options will be constrained by the services offered by spe-cific vendors.

Stages of Open Source Projects

Based on experience working with multiple open source projects, it's been observed that projects tend to go through common stages. Not every project goes through all of these stages, and other observers might categorize these stages differently, but for our purposes we'll categorize these stages as the *incubation stage*; the *initial release stage*; the *"curing cancer" stage*; the *broken promises stage*; the *hardening phase*; the *enterprise stage*; and, finally, a *terminal stage*. In the following sections we explain each of these stages to help you in identifying where a project is in its lifespan, which will help determine how you should evaluate that project as a solution.

As you read through these project life-cycle stages, you might notice parallels to the *Gartner Hype Cycle*, which is a methodology created by Gartner, Inc. to track the maturity of technologies. The following are the stages of the Hype Cycle and how they relate to the project stages we use in this chapter:

Technology Trigger
    The private incubation and initial release stages

Peak of Inflated Expectations
    The "curing cancer" stage

Trough of Disillusionment
    The broken promises stage

Slope of Enlightenment
    The enterprise stage

Plateau of Productivity
    The enterprise and decline stages

Private Incubation Stage

Many successful open source projects start off as internal projects, typically sponsored by a parent company or university. The parent entity usually provides the initial funding and, just as important, it provides the problem for which the project is intended to solve. There are many great examples of this: much of Apache Kafka was developed at LinkedIn to solve the company's data integration challenges, Apache Hive came out of Facebook to facilitate user access to data, Apache Spark came from the University of California at Berkeley, Apache Impala started life as Cloudera Impala, and the list goes on.

Many projects will go through an external incubation phase after the internal incubation, but there are many benefits as well as some pitfalls to the internal incubation phase. An internal incubation phase provides the opportunity to set the direction of the project and establish a consistent architecture and style for developers to follow as well as time to build a solid codebase, create documentation, and so forth. This also provides an opportunity to create a clear story for the value that the project provides and the technical problems it addresses—even for open source, software marketing is critical.

Given that this incubation phase is invisible to most of us, why even bring it up in a discussion on evaluating open source projects? The reason is the importance of this stage to the success of a project—projects that navigate the incubation stage well have a much higher chance of succeeding in the long run. Support from the parent entity will likely be the driving force behind the project for the first couple of years.

Release Stage

This is the moment right after the project has become open, and there are a number of important things we can learn about a project on its release:

How much support and momentum does the project have?
> Are there blog posts, articles, and so on announcing the release of the project? Is it given session time at industry conferences? Or is it simply released with little notice or impact? Additionally, does the sponsoring entity have a good reputation and track record for supporting projects? Similarly, do the core developers on the project have good reputations?

What's the positioning and vision for the project?
> Does the project have a clear story of the technical problems it's trying to address? This is important because this will play a big role in the direction the project will take and its chances for adoption.

Is the project evolutionary or revolutionary?
> When a project first comes out, we need to judge it in comparison with projects that claim to solve the same or similar problems. Is this project a major advancement from previous solutions or just incrementally better? We ask this question because of the energy and resources required to switch technologies. An incremental change is often not worth the cost of switching. We need to ask ourselves whether the existing projects in the market can adapt to the limitations addressed by this newly announced project, or is the gap so wide and the benefit so great that this new project is changing the game in such a way that existing projects won't be able to compete?

"Curing Cancer" Stage

For better or worse, most major projects have gone through a stage we can refer to as the "curing cancer" stage. In this stage, our new project is selling itself aggressively, with a focus on (and sometimes overexaggerating) the benefits provided by the project. You know a project is in this stage when you see the following:

- The project promises an easy solution to every problem.
- There is little talk of limitations or issues with the project.
- There's a great deal of interest and demand by technology workers to use the project without a clear idea of how the project can deliver value.

This stage is actually important to an open source project. Without this hype, projects likely wouldn't get the number of committers and contributors they need to get through to the next stage. Projects would also probably not garner enough adoption to be able to move to the next stages.

So as a decision maker, how should you consider projects in this stage? The best advice is to treat these projects with cautious optimism. Take care to fully evaluate the project to determine whether it can provide a solution to your problem or is just hype. The guidance provided later in this chapter in the section "Considerations for Technology Selection" on page 41 can also provide value when evaluating projects in this stage.

Another option is simply to wait a while. This can often be your best option because as a project or technology becomes more mature, the time to value decreases. This happens for a number of reasons: fewer bugs, more examples and documentation, more people trained in the technology, and less FUD (fear, uncertainty, and doubt) to contend with.

Unless your company is in the business of being on the cutting edge, when a project is in this state it makes sense to wait for some period of time—at least 6 to 12 months—before you perform a serious evaluation. You will find your path to success is smoother if you just wait for others to hit all the bumps first. Also, waiting can get you to the goal faster and with a better architecture than the early adopters because you'll be starting with a stronger foundational knowledge.

Broken Promises Stage

After the hype, most projects run into reality. In general, if you haven't experienced some type of broken promise related to your open source project of choice, you haven't used it enough. Reality often intrudes when the following occurs:

Opening up to new users
When a project is released to a larger user base beyond the project developers and experienced users, issues and limitations with the project codebase and documentation surface.

Running at scale
Regardless of the level of design and architectural effort that goes into developing of a system, it's difficult to fully model the types of workloads that a project will face in the real world. It's very common for projects to run into scalability issues when subject to production workloads. In the worst case, the software might require major rewrites or architectural overhauls to meet these unexpected scale demands.

Security
It's common for security to take a back seat to functional considerations with many open source projects. This is not necessarily a failing of the project; rather, it's a pragmatic choice focused on solving problems as expediently as possible. This of course becomes an issue if the project grows into an enterprise solution and can result in major efforts to incorporate security into the system.

Auditability and maintainability

These are also critical to an enterprise solution, but like security, they can often be an afterthought in the initial development of an open source project. Many open source projects targeted at an enterprise market are getting better at this, but this is still an area where significant gaps might exist that need to be filled.

Integration

There might be limitations in the solution that make integrating the solution with existing systems and architectures challenging.

The broken promises stage is the make-or-break point for most open source projects. Will the project survive and overcome the issues that surface, or will these issues be too great from which to recover?

Note that this phase is a required part of any successful project; it's almost certain that any solution you'll be evaluating will have gone through this stage. Even if a project is currently in this stage, it shouldn't be viewed as a disqualifier. If a project has reached this stage, it means that people are using the project, finding issues, understanding limitations, and so on. This is all necessary for a project to move to the hardening stage, which we discuss next.

Finally, note that this stage provides an opportunity for adopters to have an influential role in the community and help subsequent users as the project advances.

Hardening Stage

This is where the exciting early development turns into pragmatic, incremental development. This stage isn't nearly as exciting, but it's required if a project is going to be able to gain widespread adoption in the enterprise.

In this stage of a project, the focus will be on things like auditing, security, and resilience. Fortunately, as we've seen in a number of projects, you usually can add these features at a later stage without having to redesign the solution. The main headache for users will be the speed with which these features are added—all of these features are complex and require a good deal of oversight from within the project.

Another thing that makes this stage interesting is that the original development team of the project might not be the team that is doing the hardening. As projects mature, the founders and early developers might move on to other roles and projects. As long as the project has established a solid community and a healthy ecosystem, this can be a healthy transition and not a cause for concern. In fact, if a project outlives its original developers, this can be a good sign of the success of the project.

In many cases, you will begin to see projects at this stage relying on two groups of resources: a group of committers focused on hardening, and another group focused on innovation. This latter group is still trying to push the boundaries of what the software can do and hopefully increase its scope, whereas the more pragmatic group is trying to make the software enterprise ready today.

As time goes on, the hardening group will mostly likely grow, whereas the innovation group will shrink. It's in the nature of this innovator group to move on to subprojects or new projects that provide more freedom and speed of development.

Keep in mind that both groups are important and there needs to be a balance. Keep an eye on the following factors:

Balance
>   If we don't have continual innovation, the project will be out-of-date sooner than desired. If we don't have pragmatic development, the software will never work in production.

Technical debt
>   The longer it takes a project to get to the hardening stage or the longer a project keeps its focus on innovation, the more technical debt builds up. At some point, this technical debt is not worth the cost to pay down, and the project will die.

Who should you partner with and trust?
>   During this stage, there might be parts of a project that are stable and other parts that are unstable. Should you align your company with the innovators or the pragmatists? Although both will agree the project has great potential, they might have differing views for where the project is suitable. You need to listen to both, but if you intend to deploy this product, you need to turn your attention to the pragmatists. You can listen to the dreamers but only to understand the possibilities and future direction.

Enterprise Stage

Many projects never reach this stage, given the challenges of moving through the previous stages. It's easy to see whether a product has reached this stage: it will likely be successfully deployed in production across a number of companies. Deployment at organizations that had little to no involvement in the development of the project is important because it tells us several things:

The software is supportable and maintainable
>   If the companies deploying it aren't the driving forces behind the development of the project, this means that there are companies or efforts outside the parent organization providing support for the software.

The software is stable
>   A particularly strong sign of stability of a project is when it's in production at financial services companies because these companies have a lot to lose if they're working with unstable technologies.

The pragmatists outnumber the innovators
> Normally by this stage, the members of the pragmatic group have outnumbered those in the innovator group. This indicates a demand for stability because the existing product already meets the needs of the market and there is less demand for new features.

Many notable examples of data management systems have reached the enterprise stage, including Apache Hadoop, Apache Cassandra, Apache Kafka, and so on.

Decline and Slow Death Stage

The last stage of an open source project is a little depressing. It is extremely rare that projects are declared dead or are completely shut down; instead, development slows down to the point where innovation stops.

A major reason projects enter this stage is that they are no longer the market leader for the given use case. This could be because the project was out-innovated, the underlying hardware assumptions of the project have changed, or the codebase and project politics produced an environment that prevented needed innovation.

If your project reaches this stage, it doesn't necessarily mean that it's time to begin looking for other solutions—remember that people are still using mainframes! The main thing is to understand how the project got to this stage and study the market to look for other projects that might show value for future use cases or reimplementation of existing use cases.

Another important consideration is the importance of the solution to your architecture. If the project serves as the core of your architecture, you might want to more carefully consider the timetable to retire that system. On the other hand, if it plays a smaller part, transitioning to a new solution might make more sense.

Common Life Cycles for Open Source Projects

With the major stages now defined, it is time to talk about exceptions. Not all open source projects will follow the full life cycle that we just described. It's important to understand why a project would follow a different path because it can affect our understanding of the current state of the project.

Before going into the exceptions, let's review the default path for an open source project, as shown in Figure 2-1.

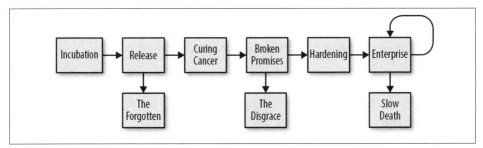

Figure 2-1. Default open source project life cycle

Let's take a closer look at each of the stages in the life cycle:

Incubation

Building up momentum as an internal project with the help of the parent organization.

Release

Becoming an open source project.

The Forgotten

The sad fact is that most open source projects, although started with the best of intentions, never gain widespread adoption and are quickly forgotten.

Curing Cancer

The hype (most likely over-hype) used to get external use of the project and to get more interest that will result in additional contributors.

Broken Promises

When people not initially involved in the project begin using the project and the reality of the project's shortcomings emerge.

The Disgrace

Successful projects are able to use the broken promises stage as a springboard to a more solid project. Some projects, unable to overcome these issues, are abandoned and forgotten.

Hardening

The long process of addressing the shortcomings of the project such as auditability, security, and failover.

Enterprise

The most productive years of the project—at this stage, the project has lost most of its hype and most people have a good understanding of what the project can do as well as the situations for which it's not suited.

Decline and Slow Death
> The last stage of an open source project life, when contributions begin to slow and interest moves away from the project toward new technologies.

With the default life cycle defined, let's review some of the alternative life cycles of which you should be mindful.

Open Sourcing a Dead Product

Recent years have seen a shift by companies away from proprietary solutions toward open source, and not just in the big data space. Open source software provides advantages for companies, such as lower cost and reduced vendor lock-in. A side effect of this is that some products that have been established in the market for a while begin to lose market share to open source projects. One approach to try to counter this is to relaunch the product, sometimes under a new name, as open source in the hopes of reviving the product's market share.

This (arguably) rarely works in practice for several reasons:

The product's market share was already drying up
> A strong product that still provides value to companies will continue to find market share. If not, companies are likely going to look for more capable solutions.

Closed source is built very differently from an open source project
> There are coding practices and cultural differences between commercial and open source software. It can be difficult to bridge these differences when moving from one model to the other.

It's difficult to let go
> Often, when trying to open source a product, it is difficult for the parent organization to let go of control, which is required to attract outside developers. A couple of ways to open up a project without giving up control are to release only a part of the product to open source or release the code in a publicly accessible repository such as GitHub, as opposed to contributing to an organization such as the Apache Software Foundation.

The solution is just old hat
> Excitement in the open source world comes a lot from new ideas, which is unlikely with an older product.

These issues will result in a different life cycle from the default one. In this case, the life cycle will look more like that shown in Figure 2-2.

Figure 2-2. Life cycle for open sourcing a dead product

The Follower

Although companies can often lower costs with open source software, a considerable amount of money is being made in the open source market. For this reason, it's common to see competing projects that aim to gain market share from the leader—we refer to these as "followers," although a more charitable term might be "competitor." A follower will normally market itself as better than the leader because it addresses functionality that the leader left out. The follower's life cycle will look more like that illustrated in Figure 2-3.

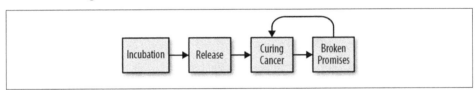

Figure 2-3. Follower project life cycle

The follower might remain in the curing cancer stage for a long time. This is because it has a difficult time getting the adoption of the leader and therefore doesn't get to the broken promises stage.

Should we look at followers? The answer is, maybe; these projects might warrant some attention, but you should watch to see if they reach—and begin to break out of —the broken promises stage. It's especially important to be cautious with these types of projects, given that many of them tend to be short-lived. Additionally, a follower project might just have a history of taking ideas and implementations from the leader, in which case the project will have little chance of overtaking the leader in the long term.

Although we've painted a somewhat negative picture, there are definitely examples of projects that could be classified as followers that have grown to be successful projects and could even be viewed as leaders in their own right. A good example is Apache Flink, which initially seemed to be trying to fill the same niche as Spark insomuch as it offered similar APIs. However, over time Flink was able to differentiate itself as a useful tool for a number of use cases, particularly in stream processing. Although Spark is probably stronger as a batch-processing engine versus Flink, there are functional and performance benefits for stream-processing applications provided by Flink that make it well worth exploring as an alternative to Spark Streaming.

Additionally, in some cases leaders have been eclipsed by the followers, and the followers should probably be considered over the earlier projects. An example of this might be Apache Storm, which for a long time was viewed as a strong contender for stream-processing applications, but in recent years has seen decreasing usage and activity in favor of more recent solutions such as Spark Streaming. Even though competitors such as Spark Streaming and Flink seem to be thriving, Storm now appears to be an example of a project in the slow death stage.

Evaluating Benchmarks

Regardless of where a project is in the life cycle, it's inevitable that there will be considerable noise around performance comparisons or benchmarks. As you probably already know, there can be some value in these benchmarks, but they need to be viewed with a great deal of skepticism.

On the plus side, benchmarks can tell us a lot about which technologies are competing for the same market and give some idea to how they compare. On the other hand, many factors can affect the validity of benchmarks:

Mistakes based on incomplete knowledge or methodologies
It's possible that the folks performing the testing don't have a sufficient understanding of the software to give them a fair shot in all the tests. Although the testers might be making an honest attempt to perform a fair test, these misunderstandings or flawed methodologies lead to invalid results. For example, testers might not have the experience and knowledge to provide the same level of tuning for all of the tools involved in the testing. Another example might be when evaluating competitive products.

Hidden biases
Unconscious biases can lead to poor test methodologies, improper tuning of competing products, and so on that could inadvertently lead to invalid results.

Motivated biases
In some cases, invalid testing due to biases might not be inadvertent, and tests are intentionally structured to provide an advantage to a particular tool. This can especially be the case when the organization performing the testing has a stake in the tests results.

Unfair comparison
It's common to see benchmarks that compare two tools but only with use cases or workloads for which one tool has an advantage.

Despite these caveats, benchmarks can provide value in the following areas:

Understanding markets
Benchmarks can tell us which projects are comparable. This allows us to see how the market is shaping up.

Determining market leaders
If you see multiple benchmarks comparing against a single tool, that could be a good indication that the tool is the market leader.

Testing scripts
A good benchmark will share the code, configurations, and testing data used in the test. You can use this to validate the test independently. If you're evaluating a benchmark that doesn't publish these things, you should consider the benchmark results to be extremely questionable. It's important to hold benchmarks to an open standard of repeatability and verification.

As a final note on benchmarks, it's important for you to perform internal benchmarks with your use cases and data. Sometimes your use case is unique, and published benchmarks don't apply. Often, you can engage with vendors or outside experts to provide assistance with configuration, tuning, and so on for the different tools you intend to compare.

Considerations for Technology Selection

We discussed the open source project life cycle and the realities of benchmarking, so how can you apply this to your technology selection process? Before providing the answer, let's go through some factors that can motivate and influence your decisions:

Business needs
The specific use cases and requirements you've been tasked to implement.

Internal demand
Your teams want new challenges and to learn new technologies.

Desire to live on the edge
You want to be seen as a pioneer in your company.

Risk tolerance
You want to avoid failure and public embarrassment.

Stress tolerance
You want clear sailing from development to production. No one wants to be on a support call at 1:00 A.M. because of unknown issues.

Skill gap
> You want to pick a technology set that your staff will be able to master based on their skill levels.

With these factors in mind, we can use the business need to define a scope that will help us isolate which tools are relevant for our selection process. This process will take into account things like features, cost, and scalability. The following sections provide guidance on performing further evaluation of solutions selected as part of this process.

Understanding the Building Blocks

Technology moves quickly, but new systems more often than not are built on existing architectures and concepts. Consider Apache Kafka; although Kafka can provide higher throughput for large volumes of events than previous systems, at its core it's really a distributed log that borrows concepts from traditional publish–subscribe messaging systems.

This is arguably an oversimplification, but the point is that to understand a complex technology, it's helpful to first break it down and then take those parts and compare them to systems that we already understand. This process can help us understand the possible limits and benefits of a system before any hands-on experience. Even with what seems like a completely new system, the fundamentals still apply.

Evaluating Major Components of Big Data Solutions

To provide a little more detail, the following provides examples of what to look for when evaluating big data solutions, broken out by some major components. This is not meant to be an exhaustive list, but just intended to give you some ideas on the things to look for when evaluating technology solutions.

Storage System Components:

Relative location of data to the reader
> Where does data reside in relation to consumers of the data? As an example to illustrate this, until relatively recently, data locality was central to the architecture of Hadoop Distributed File System (HDFS). In today's world of cloud and dynamic compute resources, there is a shift to move to remote storage. There are benefits to both architectural approaches, so you need to evaluate this in the context of your use cases and requirements.

Compression formats and rates
> Not all systems compress the same way. They might use similar compression codecs, but the format of the precompressed data can have a huge impact on the compression.

Data structures
> How the data is laid out has huge impacts on access patterns and storage cost. Chapter 5 offers a broader discussion on storage systems.

Partitioning, replication, and failure
> There are only so many models for distributed systems in terms of partitioning, replication, and failure recovery. Categorize your solution and compare the pros and cons of its offering versus your use cases.

API and interfaces
> This will be your main window into your storage system. Make sure it's friendly with systems you plan to use. Otherwise, you might have a great storage system that's unusable.

Processing engines:

Resource allocation
> This will greatly affect the scalability of the system as well as the ability of the system to support multiple users at the same time.

Shuffling and optimizer approaches
> One of the main value drivers a distributed execution system offers you is the ability to optimize jobs and move the data around for different reasons. You should categorize and compare this with other tools.

Categorization of use cases
> Different execution engines might focus on different use cases, optimizing for one over the other.

API and interfaces
> Again, the system must be easy to use and accessible with the tools you already have.

Looking to a Guide for Advice

As a technology decision maker, you're almost certainly aware that there is no magic bullet. But even the most experienced technologist can benefit from outside guidance. Working with consultants or analysts can be helpful—these are often people who have seen technologies come and go and can provide a more clear-eyed vision of technological direction.

Using Analysts

Industry analysts such as Gartner or Forrester Research are another potential source of guidance in helping to evaluate and select solutions. You can access their findings either via the reports that these organizations produce or through personal meetings with analysts. Generally speaking, these analysts generate their products through meetings with vendors and customers, although in some cases the analysts will perform hands-on testing. This process can provide these analysts with a broad view of a market, including the current state of the market, which tools are leading the market, and how those tools are being utilized by companies.

Although this process can yield valuable insights and make analysts a valuable resource, the fact remains that in many cases analysts are generating data based on conversations with vendors and customers, and not actual experience running products. Needless to say, this can lead to flawed inputs. For example, even though it's expected that vendors will have a strong bias toward their own offerings, customers also might not be able to objectively evaluate their own decisions and instead work to defend their technology choices.

Analysts are, of course, also subject to biases, both conscious and unconscious. This can be the result of vendor misinformation, relationships with vendors or customers, or simply insufficient knowledge or time. It's also not uncommon to see purportedly objective reports written by analysts that are actually engaged with a specific vendor.

So, although you view analysts as valuable resources, remember to treat their output as another variable in a comprehensive evaluation process.

Looking to Market Trends

So far, we've discussed some fairly subjective resources for evaluating projects, but we can also look to some trends for more objective measures of a project:

Community interest
> Looking at the number of user groups and meetups (and their attendance levels) organized around a solution can provide a good gauge of the level of interest in a technology.

Google trends
> Google trends can also be a good measure of the level of interest in projects or technologies.

GitHub activity
> GitHub can tell us a lot about the interest and activity for a project. For example, look at the number of contributors, number of commits, and so on. An active and thriving project will have a high level of recent and ongoing activity. If GitHub seems overly quiet with respect to a particular project, proceed with caution.

Jira count
> Related to GitHub activity, activity on an open source project's issue-tracking system (this is generally Jira nowadays) can provide useful insights. For example, looking at the number of issues over the past 30 days, both open and closed, can be telling. Just go to any open source project and look at its past 30 days of activ-

ity. Normally, more activity means more interest and hardening/features being done for a project. You also want to see how many companies are involved with the project. This will give you a real look into who is using the technology and the diversity of the committer base.

Email lists and community forums

Any active project will have thriving email distribution lists and/or online forums. Watch for activity in these venues; is engagement growing or trending down?

Conferences and user groups

Here again, a thriving project will have associated events where people are meeting to talk about the project. This might be conference sessions or even dedicated conferences, or an active user group community. Whereas conferences tend to be hosted and sponsored by vendors, look for meetups that have been created by developers and users, as opposed to vendors trying to promote products.

Contributors

Who's contributing to the project? Ideally, there's a diverse group and representation from multiple companies. Be cautious if a single company dominates development on a project.

Follow the money

Last but not least is the money trail. How well attended are the conferences? If the companies are public, what do their growth trends look like? Are there competitors in the market, and how healthy are they?

After narrowing our selections, we need to look at factors like demand, internal skill levels, risk tolerance, and how willing we are to be on the cutting edge. These factors will be personal to your team—you want a solution that your staff and organization will be proud of and happy to work with.

Then, test out the solutions before fully committing. Keep in mind that you're not bound to just one selection—you can pick more than one solution for evaluation and compare the initial development and progress. If you make a choice that isn't meeting the requirements of your use case or presents challenges in development, don't be afraid to change course and pursue other solutions.

Summary

As with any technology selection process, selecting a big data solution requires that you first define these critical items:

- What are the requirements of your project?
- What are the existing skill sets within your organization?

- What's your level of tolerance for risk?

- What's your timeline, budget, and so on?

Answering these questions will facilitate the selection of a solution and universally apply, no matter whether you're evaluating open source or commercial solutions. Additionally, many of the same resources that can be used when selecting a commercial technology (e.g., analysts, conferences, and peers) apply when selecting open source projects.

However, in the open source world, it's important to have an understanding of the life cycle of projects in order to be able to thoroughly evaluate a particular solution. Also, just as for commercial solutions, it's important to be able to critically evaluate vendor claims and benchmarks when making decisions.

The focus in this chapter has been on the software selection process and general considerations. Chapter 3 covers reducing risk *after* you have made your selection.

CHAPTER 3

Managing Risk in Data Projects

Humans excel at worrying about things, but normally we worry about the wrong things. As a child, Ted wasted what should have been many hours of sleep on planning an escape route when zombies attacked. People fear a lot of things that, whether grounded in reality or not, will most likely never affect them. A perfect example is that people are more afraid of sharks or terrorist attacks, when the chances of dying from heart disease or a car accident are significantly higher.

This is also true when it comes to software development. Identifying what to worry about and what to not worry about is an extremely powerful practice when implementing successful projects, especially when you're working with new technologies. If managed properly, risk can be an opportunity—if everything was known at the start of a project, what would be the fun in that?

In this chapter, we discuss how to manage risk after completing the software selection process and moving on to implementing a project. The focus of this chapter is on helping you set up methodologies and an environment for success by using development principles and strategies for managing and mitigating risk, setting realistic expectations, and providing a guide to building successful teams.

Categories of Risk

Before we delve into the details of risk management, let's first talk about the broad categories of risk that we want to address in project planning.

Technology Risk

Any software project involves risk, and building large, complex distributed data solutions can increase these risks. This is especially true when those projects are based on new and unfamiliar systems. Risk can come from individual components used in implementing the architecture, interactions between components, and so on.

Risk can also come from unfamiliarity with a technology used in designing the system. Fortunately, there are strategies that we can employ to manage and mitigate these risks as we move from design to implementation of our application.

Team Risk

Team risk refers to the risk associated with the team members implementing the data architecture, as well as external teams. This risk can come from the knowledge level and strength of your team, dependencies on external teams, and even potentially disruptive team members.

Requirements Risk

A common source of requirements risk is poorly defined requirements or sometimes poorly defined problems. Another source of requirements risk, particularly with new technologies, are requirements that your team hasn't worked with before. For example, latency or throughput requirements that are higher than anything the team has built before. Scope creep can also be a common source of requirements risk.

In the next section, we go into more details on these risks types and discuss how to manage these risks.

Managing Risk

In this section, we begin with a methodology that uses a high-level model to assign risk levels to components in the system—this has worked well in practice on various projects. These risk levels encompass the different types of risk we discussed in the previous section and provide a framework to quantify and address these risks.

Categorizing Risk in Your Architecture

This approach starts by breaking the architecture into pieces. Figure 3-1 shows an example of breaking apart a common data storage and processing system.

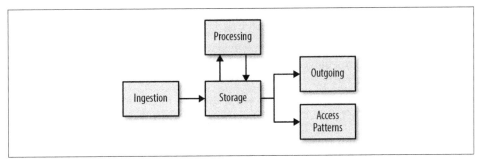

Figure 3-1. Breaking an architecture into high-level components

In Figure 3-1, we have an example of breaking up a system into data ingest, data serving, data processing, access patterns, and storage. We can drill down even further to subcomponents within these components, as shown in Figure 3-2.

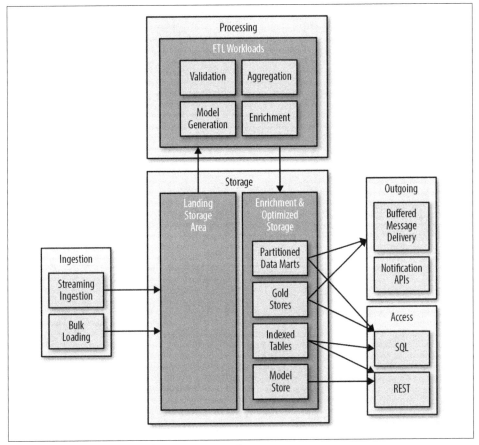

Figure 3-2. Breaking an architecture into subcomponents

At this stage, we likely won't want to go any deeper in breaking down the system. After we've reached this level, we want to define interfaces to each subcomponent. This will help mitigate the risk of failure in one subsystem affecting the rest of the system. (We examine the subject of interface design later in this chapter.) For now, just think about this as a system of self-contained components that you can develop independently from the others, and that allows the risk of each component to be contained within that component.

The next step is to begin assigning which technologies you're going to use to implement components, as illustrated in Figure 3-3. You can then assign team members to work on each component and then apply risk weights to the technologies and to development teams; we discuss this process shortly, starting with technology risk.

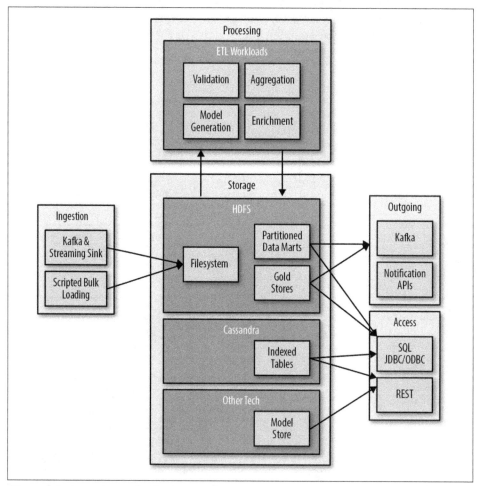

Figure 3-3. Assigning technologies to subcomponents

Figure 3-3 shows that we've made technology selections, including the following:

Kafka
For buffered streaming of data.

Hadoop Distributed File System (HDFS) and object storage
For initial landing zones and long-term storage for data.

Cassandra
For high-performance indexed storage.

Other
This is a placeholder for things like in-memory databases and search-based systems such as Elasticsearch.

For now, you can view these technology selections as placeholders; we dig into detailed reasons to select one technology over another in later chapters. For example, we talk in more detail about storage layer options in Chapter 5, and data processing options in Chapter 8. The main idea here is to have technology selection defined within the initial design, with the knowledge that if the technology is determined to be unsuitable, we can just swap it out. Let's go through an example.

Suppose that you select a NoSQL like Cassandra or HBase to be the base store for a time-series database. Everything works fine initially, but you run into issues as you move along in the life cycle of the project; for example:

- Cassandra can't store enough data on any given node, and the price becomes an issue.
- HBase or Cassandra background processing (e.g., compaction) of data starts to affect performance.
- Query time aggregation is turning out to be too expensive as the number of unique metrics reaches a certain point.
- Performance is fine, but pricing with a vendor becomes a concern.

So, there could be a number of reasons why your initial technology selection doesn't work out, but fortunately if you follow our recommendations in Chapter 4 on using interfaces in your architecture, you can make these changes without causing significant disruption to your design.

Technology Risk

Risk weighting for a team or technology is not an exact science, but normally gut feeling can go a long way. For example, if you have used a given technology in production before and your team has considerable experience, that technology should have a lower risk rating. Conversely, you should, of course, assign a technology with which you have little or no experience a higher risk rating.

Also, knowing a technology involves many levels of knowledge. As an example, consider SQL. Your team can have years of experience with SQL but might not have a lot of experience with SQL on newer "big data" query engines like Hive, Spark SQL, Cassandra CQL, or Impala. Not all query engines behave the same way, and different engines might or might not support specific SQL features. Understanding these capabilities and limitations is key to using one of these systems and extending beyond just knowing the query language. When we say that we know a technology, we need to know it from top to bottom.

Sometimes, the Best Tool Is the One You Already Know

Keep in mind that there are almost always multiple tools to solve a particular problem. As Chapter 1 discusses, often one of these tools might be one that you're already using. If multiple organizations, including your own, are having success with a tool, it seems like a safe bet that the tool is a solid choice for your architecture.

The important question is how well your team understands the tool, as well as the requirements of your project. This will help in understanding if the tool is a good choice for your application. A hammer is great for driving nails into a wall. It can also serve as a can opener but is definitely not optimal for that task, and it's not so good at washing windows.

In short, knowing your tools and what they are good for is key to being successful with those tools.

Strength of the Team

Next, we should look at the risk level of a team. This will come down to your personal knowledge of the abilities of team members as well as the team's history of completing tasks and meeting deadlines. If you're working with new resources or less-experienced team members, that will likely mean a higher risk weighting for that team.

Of course, regardless of experience levels, each team has different types of people with different skill sets. The following describes some of the types typical of development teams, and a well-rounded team should have at least some of the following personalities:

The cleaner
> This person has a meticulous attention to detail and will ensure that the project has complete test coverage, code is fully version controlled, and so on.

The prototyper

This person is not afraid to experiment and investigate new software. Their role is to test out approaches and hit risk areas before it is too late to alter the design or approach.

The workhorse

These folks serve a critical role because they are the ones who will get most of the work done.

The highly flexible

These are the people who are always eager to learn and grow and are able to adapt quickly. These folks can facilitate bringing the rest of the team along as the project progresses.

The negotiator

Dealing with project management or external groups is an important task. Not all developers enjoy this style of communication. It takes a special resource to be able to both understand technology and understand how to work across teams to deliver projects.

Additionally, certain personality types are potential red flags for your team and can have direct impacts on your project risk:

The "cowboy" coder

Anyone who's worked in technology for any period of time is familiar with this type—these are the developers who prefer to go their own way and work on their own. This type is often a very efficient and talented programmer but also not generally a good team player. They can typically get more work done than your average programmer, but often this work won't follow coding standards or be well documented. Sometimes the cowboy can be an asset, but often their inability to work with a team and conform to standards or processes becomes more of a liability.

The toxic personality

Every so often a team will have a member who, sometimes inadvertently, is disruptive to the team dynamics. This can be caused by a number of factors—sometimes these people are argumentative or are convinced they know the best way to do everything. The paradox is that these are often talented and productive individuals, but their impact on team morale and productivity outweighs these talents. Avoid these types—even less talented folks are better as long as they fit well within your team. If avoidance isn't an option, it's important that you ensure that you learn how to manage them.

In addition, it's good to have enough team members so that there are at least two people on each component. In addition to ensuring better coverage for components, having team members be accountable to someone else can often produce better outcomes.

Other Teams

In addition to the risk associated with the project team, there's also the risk of interacting with one or more external groups. This is particularly true if those groups are working on components or systems that are critical to the work of your team or, conversely, where the work of your team is important to the success of external teams. Whenever your success is directly tied to another group, be mindful and respectful. Having well-defined responsibilities and requirements is important to help achieve this. Additionally, well-defined and documented software interfaces can be key when designing software that needs to interact with systems developed by other teams.

We talk more about interfaces later in this chapter as well as in Chapter 5.

Requirements Risk

After team risk and technology risk, we have the risk level of requirements. This risk can come in different ways. One way is if requirements are vaguely defined, which might mean that later adjustments are needed that can introduce new risks. Another way is if there are requirements that your team hasn't worked with before; for example, service-level agreements or latency goals.

Having good functional requirements can help address these risks. If these functional requirements are treated as a contract that are not technology specific, they can be very effective in keeping the project on the correct path. We discuss some additional approaches to reduce requirements risk later in this chapter.

Breaking requirements into more manageable chunks of work is another way to address requirements risk. As an example of what we mean here, at a client site, one of the authors was presented with a hundred-page requirements document for a processing component. The source of this document turned out to be a previous consulting group that had been brought in to help implement a solution. As it turned out, that consulting group had failed. The approach of "boiling the ocean" taken by this requirements document created a situation in which the client was overwhelmed and unsure where to start; even though the document captured the requirements, it did not facilitate a practical development timeline or help in prioritizing requirements and task. Needless to say, that document was discarded.

After discarding the existing requirements document, the process that was followed was to build high-level requirements that could fit into a single page, along with a big-picture diagram of the intended solution. Figure 3-3 presents an example of such a diagram. From there, a component was identified that was of high importance, because, if implemented, it would increase confidence that the future solution would work. With this limited scope, it was possible to have a working Proof of Concept (PoC) for the selected component. Based on insight from this PoC, adjustments were made to the high-level requirements and then another component was identified for a PoC. This process repeated itself for about a month, after which a rough PoC for the entire system had been built.

The result is the risks had been identified; the development team understood the requirements at a deeper level; the customer had faith in the design; and with the knowledge learned from the PoC, realistic timelines could be estimated for deployment of a production version of the system.

Tying This All Together

To understand how this all fits together with the system model we've created, let's first recap the areas of risk we've discussed:

Technology knowledge
> What level of experience does your team have with the software being used to implement your application?

Team risk
> How experienced is your team, what personality types does your team have, dependencies on other teams, and so on?

Requirements risk
> What level of risk do your requirements have?

Assigning risk weightings

After performing an analysis of these different areas of risk, we can use this analysis to assign risk weightings to the system model we created. When we have accounted for all of the different risk weighting, we should see something that looks like Figure 3-4. Note that the figure is grayscale in the print edition, but you're encouraged to use color in your diagrams to better highlight the risk levels.

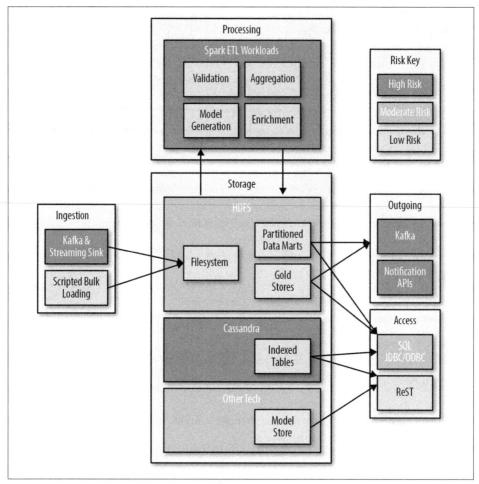

Figure 3-4. Assigning risk weightings

As you can see by the key, darker boxes indicate a higher level of risk, and lighter boxes represent a lower risk.

You should accompany this by a detailed explanation of why components are assigned a higher risk level. List each component, followed by the risk that the component and associated requirements present. If you give each risk a short title, it can quickly be referenced in discussion. Following are some examples, with each item in the list notated with the risk type we just discussed.

Cassandra

1. *Technology Experience* (technology risk): We have a limited level of experience with Cassandra within the company.

2. *Data Model* (requirements risk): We need to validate that the data model is correct for our use case.

3. *Uptime* (technology risk): We have SLA requirements that data stored in Cassandra has to be available to users with an uptime of 99.99%, which is beyond our normal SLA experience.

Bulk fetches via Spark
1. *Failure Scenario* (requirements risk): We are unsure about requirements of how to proceed when extracting data fails because of issues on the storage layer.

Kafka Streaming
1. *Technology Experience* (technology risk): This is our team's first time building streaming applications.

2. *Zero Data Loss* (technology risk): There is a requirement for zero data loss, which introduces complicated technical considerations.

Spark ETL
1. *Resource Availability* (team risk): Team members with Spark experience are already committed, which might mean assigning work to less-experienced team members.

2. *Data Model* (requirements risk): Uncertainty about the data model definition might mean having to reimplement code.

Minimizing risk

After we've estimated risk levels, we can take steps to minimize risk. Some of these steps we've already discussed, In the list that follows, we look at some of some of them in more detail:

- Lock down requirements better. As we discussed a moment ago, creating more detailed and precise functional requirements can help minimize requirements risk.

- Make sure that you share your requirements and get buy-in from all stakeholders.

- Create a clear definition of project scope and ensure stakeholder agreement.

- Add additional interface requirements and protocols with external groups. We discuss this in greater detail later, but defining strong abstractions can help reduce architectural risk by making it easier to reimplement components or replace technologies if the need arises.

- Prioritize riskier work. Tackling riskier items earlier provides additional time in case you run into problems.
- In addition to the preceding recommendation, assign riskier technologies to stronger and more experienced team members.
- Use external resources to help address knowledge gaps. You'll learn more about this later in the chapter.
- Use prototypes and PoCs to reduce architectural risk.
- Replace riskier components with less-risky ones. For example, in our hypothetical risk breakdown, we might decide to replace Spark for Extract, Transform, and Load (ETL) processing with a tool that available team members are more familiar with such as MapReduce or Hive.

Using Prototypes and Proofs of Concept

It's important to have backup plans if a component of your architecture fails to meet expectations, but this failure can affect the perceptions of your project or your schedule. What if you could fail faster before a failure becomes too impactful to projects? Let's look at some ways to do just that.

Build Two to Three Ways

The trick is simple: start with straightforward requirements that are wide in their impact and then brainstorm at least two to three ways to meet those requirements. Implement each of your solutions and then run benchmarks. This can help you to select the best of your solutions or come to a realization that you need to explore further. The key here is to build fast—think of these solutions as prototypes. You should learn several things through this process:

- The quality of the documentation of the system you're using
- Performance of the solution: throughput, latency, and so on
- Complexity of the different approaches
- The ability of the team to pick up the technology and develop their opinions of the technology

Build PoCs and Then Throw Them Away

Creating a PoC can be a valuable way to validate a technology or approach. A good way to approach a PoC is to view it as throwaway work and build it as quickly as possible. The goal is to push the requirements and technology as hard as possible within a limited window of time. After a PoC is successful, you should rewrite the code and maybe even have different developers do most of the new implementation. This will provide a couple of things:

More eyes
Again, having a different perspective can be good validation of your PoC.

Better systems
The experience and knowledge gained from building the PoC can often help in building better systems.

A common problem with PoCs that you want to avoid is management seeing it and saying "Hey, it works! Ship it." Having said this, it's useful to design PoCs that implement a minimally viable product (MVP) for production deployment. This will allow you to better evaluate the suitability of your solution.

Deployment Considerations

It wasn't too long ago that code would be deployed to servers that were manually configured, requiring long checklists of steps to upgrade or set up a new system deployment. This created considerable risk when it was necessary to deploy new code, update software, and so on because of the lack of tested, repeatable processes to manage changes. Mature organizations now use automation software, including build systems like Jenkins, configuration management systems like Puppet or Chef, and containers such as Docker to manage and automate changes to systems. By using these systems, you can considerably reduce the risk of software deployments.

Although an in-depth discussion of these systems is beyond the scope of this book, the takeaway here is that having tested and repeatable build and deployment systems and processes is key to moving fast and reducing risk. Many production issues are a result of upgrades, configuration changes, library updates, and so forth gone wrong. The more you automate your build and deployment, the more you've reduced your risk of issues occurring during deployments to production.

Using Interfaces

Interfaces are a common and important concept in software development. They provide an important tool to reduce risk in a software architecture by reducing coupling and dependencies between components. Interface design at a project or architecture level is the idea of having different parts of the application agree upon a mode of communicating to other areas of the architecture. A common implementation of this concept is a service layer implementation to serve as the interface between a frontend web application and a backend data store. You could implement this in any number of ways: a Representational State Transfer (REST) interface, a Java interface, a Scala trait, and so on.

The topic of interfaces is important enough that we devote Chapter 4 to discussing the design and implementation of flexible and maintainable interfaces. However, we want to briefly touch here on how interfaces can help to reduce risk in your projects.

So how do interfaces help to address risk? One way is by allowing teams to work independently on different parts of your system. For example, the frontend team can build a dummy implementation of the interface so that they can continue development, testing, and deploying their web application without needing to worry about the progress of the backend teams. Figure 3-5 illustrates this process.

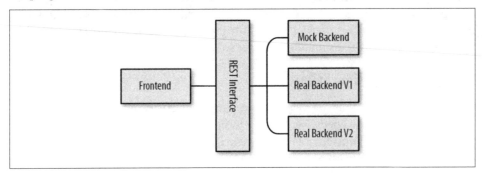

Figure 3-5. Using mock implementations with interfaces

This also means that the backend team will have the freedom to change up different strategies for storage or execution engines in their implementations without disrupting the work of the frontend team.

Using well-designed interfaces will give both the frontend and the backend teams freedom to change their designs and approaches without having to consult the other team, as long as they hold to the agreed-upon interface that they both share. You can carry out all development, load testing, unit testing, and so on without any dependencies on the other. An additional benefit of this approach can be a significant shortening of development timelines.

A good interface design can also help in communicating risk because it breaks your system into many parts, such as the following:

- Frontends
- Data ingestion and extraction
- Streaming
- Storage
- Databases
- Batch processing

- Real-time processing
- Monitoring
- Auditing
- Disaster recovery

The inherent risk of any one component will have little or no impact on the other parts. This helps in the management of risk by isolating risk to components rather than the entire project. This can provide a couple of advantages for the case in which a component is running into trouble. First, the troubled component doesn't affect the schedule of the other components. Second, when a troubled part is isolated, it provides freedom to change or even totally rewrite it as long as the interface design remains the same.

Start Building Early

Another pitfall that companies fall into is wanting to delay development until after all of the requirements are known, generally because of fears that code will be otherwise thrown away and money and time will be lost. In fact, positive things can come out of starting development as early in the process as possible:

- It will engage your development team, which will lead it to a better understanding of the requirement, which will then help the development team play a more active role in the process of requirements gathering.
- It will help flush out issues with the requirements earlier.
- It can lead to working demos. This is hugely important for two reasons: it can lower the risk level of the project by showing the outside world that real progress is being made, and it allows feedback from users. It's common for users to see a demonstration and say, "Oh, that isn't what I was thinking it would be like."
- It facilitates creating multiple designs for solving a problem and better mastery of things if an issue pops up.

Test Often and Keep Records

Often, project risk can be quantified numerically; for example, response times, concurrency, throughput, SLAs, uptime, and time to failover. It's important to ensure that you record these numbers and check and review them on a regular basis. Testing and retesting is an important part of this process.

As an example, say processing involves batch load operations that need to be tested for throughput and total execution time. To get the testing done early in the process, the team uses a data generator to create test data for input. The tests on this generated data end up giving great results, and the project used those results for sizing estimates for the entire project. Unknowingly to the team, the data that was generated just happened to have very low entropy, where entropy is a measure of how messy or different your data is from itself. More entropy means worse compression ratios, whereas lower entropy means better compression ratios. In our example, the low entropy allowed the compression codec of the execution engine to read and write data faster, send data over the wire faster, and so on.

So, when the team finally gets around to testing with real data, it's a shocking surprise to find that now the job runs much slower and the data footprint was much larger than initial testing.

We can learn the following from this example:

- Test early and test often
- Keep careful records of what was tested
- Document gaps from what was tested to what will be used in production
- Try to get your test to reflect production as much as possible
- Take any measurements with a grain of salt
- Always assume your numbers are too good to be true
- Have more than one group of people review the test processes, benchmarking, and so forth

We need to take all these items into consideration when communicating numbers to people outside our project. It is difficult to try to explain why your processing is 10 times slower today than yesterday—people will tend to be unforgiving when you try to explain the gaps after the fact.

Monitoring and Alerting

We've spent a lot of time in this chapter talking about how to plan and manage risk in your architectures, but now let's talk about managing risk beyond the implementation phases and into the deployment phase. To do this, we need a way to specify and track metrics that will allow us to ensure that the system is performing as expected after it's deployed. To define these metrics, we define key performance indicators (KPIs) for each component in the architecture. For each system, your KPIs will be different, but in general, you want to start with the three key indicators defined in the book *Site Reliability Engineering* (O'Reilly) by the folks at Google:

Throughput
    This is a measure of what your system is doing and how much of it it's doing.

Latency

This is how long it takes for your system to perform given actions.

Error rate

This is how many errors happen with respect to given operations.

The details of defining KPIs and building the required monitoring is beyond the scope of this book, but there are many references, such as the aforementioned book, that will provide in-depth information on these tasks. The main takeaway here is that without a good way to monitor information on your systems, you're operating in the dark. Defining these KPIs and building the appropriate monitoring will play an important role in reducing risk for your project after those projects have moved beyond implementation phases and through the production deployment stages.

Communicating Risk

Talking about risks is, well, risky. If you overemphasize the reality of the risks, people viewing the project from the outside will have concerns for the project that might result in unwanted and unneeded oversight. Writing software in a large company is very much like cooking in the kitchen, and oversight can be like five cooks making one sandwich. In addition, things can become even worse if politics are involved. Politics can lead to opportunists looking to take your project away. Naysayers will have reason to debate every small topic of your design, which can result in a time-suck as well as negative perceptions of the team and can inflict moral drain on the group.

There are also risks in underplaying project risk. You might need help, and if you undersell the risk and wait too long before asking for help, you risk missed deadlines, system crashes, or lost data. At this point, the result might be that you lose the project, people can lose their jobs, and your long-term effectiveness at the company could be damaged.

So, it's easy to see that if we are communicating our risks the wrong way, we are at a minimum hurting our project, and at worst it can cost us our jobs. Communication and timing are critical when talking about risk externally. This section will attempt to go into some strategies to help both communicate risk but also communicate risk in a way that protects the progression of the project.

Collaborate and Gain Buy-In

The idea here is to reduce risk by making sure that you're collaborating closely with other people within your organization. You can do this by bouncing design ideas off people, getting others to contribute to your design, and so on. By frequently bringing in others, you can benefit in multiple ways:

Having a second (or third, or fourth) pair of eyes
> Getting additional input can often provide insight and ideas that you wouldn't have come to on your own. Regardless of your level of experience and knowledge, there are benefits to seeing a design from a different perspective.

Getting buy-in
> There is no better way to get buy-in than by adopting designs or ideas of others. When others feel like their idea is part of your design, they'll feel invested in your success.

Communicate risks openly
> If you look at risks as challenging problems to solve, not only will you get others willing to help, but you might be able to enlist upper management to help solve problems outside your control or sphere of influence.

Staying in control and demonstrating progress
> Issues and risk are present in every project, but talking about risks and communicating progress in resolving the risks will demonstrate to others your team's ability to problem solve. This can increase confidence in the ability of your team to handle future risks.

Share the Risk

Related to the suggestions we just discussed, engaging with a third party such as a consultant, vendor, or trusted member from a different department can help address risk management. Assuming that the third party is highly experienced in the problems and architectures that your project will need to address, they can help in a number of ways:

- If they have experience building this type of system somewhere else, they can help you avoid pitfalls, saving you time and money.
- They can help make decisions that are unaffected by politics.
- If they are right and make your project successful, you look good.

The first item is probably the most important. The reality is that most projects require solutions that have been built by numerous other companies. Unless you're a Google, Amazon, or Facebook, your project might be a cookie-cutter implementation for the right third-party resource. If you really want to reduce risk, getting an expert to help is often a surefire way to do it.

Using Risk as a Negotiation Tool

Finally, we'll wrap things up by noting the importance of using project risk as a tool for negotiation. This might seem like a counterintuitive concept—why and how would we want to use risk for negotiations? The fact is we can sometimes use risk to facilitate project management; for example, in negotiating for more resources or modifying scope or timelines. However, it's important to be careful when selecting which risk to use for negotiations and how to use it in negotiations.

Good candidates for negotiation are risks that are linked to a business requirement. It's very important that this is a hard link to provide a solid basis for negotiation.

A good example would be if the business is asking to store terabytes of data and be able to access any of it in milliseconds. However, the company is used to using only a system like MySQL as a datastore, which is not suited for this type of use case. Suppose that the company decides to use a NoSQL store that can handle this use case, but the team doesn't have a lot of experience with the NoSQL solution. That lack of experience is a risk, but it is a risk directly brought on by a business request.

So, with a risk that is linked to a business request, we can ask for several things in project planning, such as the following:

- Additional time in the project plan
- Additional funding for a third-party expert
- More budget for hiring, training, and so forth

Note that there are cautions with this tactic: This might set expectations higher if it's assumed that the risk will go away if management provides the requested items. Additionally, if you continually make requests, the business might doubt your ability or the ability of the team to deliver a solution. So be judicious in the requests you make and ensure that you make requests with clear insight on what you need to complete the project. In the worst case, the business cancels the project because of perceived risk of failure.

Thus, with any negotiation, know what you can ask for and what you need. Be honest as much as possible; lying in either direction will most likely catch up with you.

Summary

We've used this chapter to cover the risks you need to manage in your data projects. We then discussed how to address and minimize these risks. The types of risk we discussed were as follows:

Architectural risk
> The risk that's embodied in your technology selections, how those technologies are designed to create a solution, and so forth.

Team risk
> The risks that are represented by your project teams and external teams.

Requirements risk

This risk can come from poorly defined requirements, requirements that are new to the team, and so forth.

We then discussed methods to address these risks, including the following:

- Creating a high-level model of your system to assign risk levels based on composites of these risk types
- Addressing technology and architectural risks, including use of abstractions, PoCs, and so forth
- Ensuring the creation of strong teams and addressing challenges working with external teams
- Ensuring the creation of solid and manageable requirements
- Using outside resources to help ensure project success

We also discussed the very important topic of communicating risk as well as using risk as a negotiating tool. Making sure that you've documented your risks, and a plan to manage and mitigate those risks will be critical to the success of your data projects.

CHAPTER 4

Interface Design

Building data projects with large volumes of multistructured data is complex. In addition, there's the potential complexity of integrating various components and technologies into a solution, supporting large numbers of concurrent users and different processing patterns, plus the need to be flexible in order to adapt to changing requirements and technologies.

So, how can we address these challenges when designing our systems? Well-designed interfaces can help build solutions that are maintainable, scalable, and resilient to change. In this chapter, we focus on what makes a good interface design, some nonfunctional considerations, and some common interface examples.

The Human Body

Before going into technology, let's reflect on a system that's far more complex than any we're likely to ever build. This system also uses interfaces and very focused subsystems to reduce dependencies and adapt to changing conditions over time (although somewhat larger time spans than our systems will have to deal with). The system we're referring to is the human body; if we think of it as a collection of high-level parts connected by interfaces, we can identify parallels to our own systems.

The Human Body Versus a Data Architecture

If we look at the main systems in the human body, we can begin to note some interesting parallels to a modern data architecture. Let's take a look at some of these parallels, starting with the body's peripheral nervous system and central nervous system.

Peripheral nervous system

The first major component we're looking at is the network of information pipes that connect all the components in the body, allowing them to send and receive data with other components. This is our peripheral nervous system (PNS), the nerves that span our body and receive input from all of our senses. The PNS sends this input to our brain and sends commands out to other systems like muscles, instructing them to take actions. Think of this as the information superhighway of the body.

Distributed data systems have a number of similarities, with the clearest example being *publish–subscribe* (pub–sub) systems like Kafka. We talk more about pub–sub later in this chapter. For now, we can define pub–sub simply as a system that has publishers that publish data to a central broker, and subscribers that consume that data for further processing. If we look at Kafka in a data architecture, it will look something like Figure 4-1. In this example, Kafka is accepting information from external streams or sensors and sending to storage systems or near-real-time (NRT) processing systems where we can make decisions based on the data. These decisions then can travel back through Kafka and be sent to services that can take action based on commands generated from the decisions.

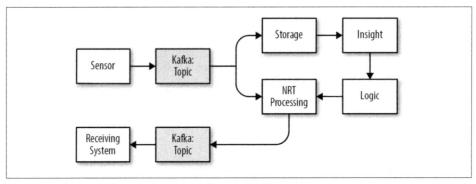

Figure 4-1. Data architecture compared to the PNS

Central nervous system

As shown in Figure 4-2, the central nervous system (CNS) is composed of the more purposeful parts of your nervous system like your brain and your spinal cord. These are systems that have more-complex jobs than just transporting information. These systems can be further broken down into subsystems that have specific functions; for example, the brain is composed of different lobes such as the occipital lobe, which provides visual processing functions; the frontal lobe, which controls a number of functions such as memory and language; and so on. These systems also control other systems in the body, such as muscles and the heart.

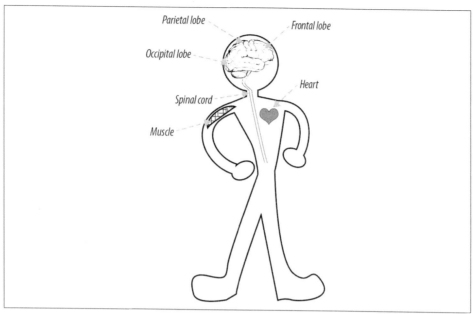

Figure 4-2. Central nervous system

If we relate this back to our big data architecture, the brain is the highlighted areas in Figure 4-3. Specifically, the brain represents the storage, NRT processing, insight, and logic components.

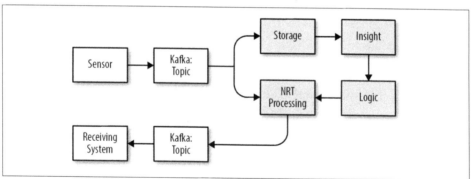

Figure 4-3. Data architecture compared to the PNS

Let's take a minute and dig into each one of these systems and how they relate to the brain:

Storage

Just as the brain has long-term and short-term memory, our data architecture has a number of data storage systems with different times to live (TTL). Additionally, our storage can be indexed in multiple ways, just as our brain uses different patterns to store and retrieve data.

Insight

This can be compared to the reflective thought in our brains that processes input and applies analysis to drive decision-making processes. In data systems, this can be related to the analysis performed via tools like SQL and machine learning.

Logic

Just as our brains arrive at decisions based on analysis of inputs and applying rules, our data systems will often have subsystems that serve the same functions.

NRT processing

This can be related to the parts of the brain that react quickly to external stimuli and drive responses. There are even some actions that happen with so little thought we call them "muscle memory" actions. The more the logic is baked into the CNS, the faster the system can process responses to input. In our data systems, we can make a comparison to systems like stream-processing engines in which we can perform complex machine learning logic and make decisions with low-millisecond response times.

Senses

The input systems like eyes, skin, and ears help us gather information about the outside world. The actual perception of the world is done in the CNS, which leaves the sensory systems as decoupled systems focused only on information gathering. Additionally, these sensors use the PNS to distribute information.

In our data architectures, the equivalent to senses are anything that generates data. These could be agents on a node, systems that input application logs, or sensors in devices. In our diagram, these would be the sensors in the highlighted box shown in Figure 4-4 that feed information to our Kafka pipes.

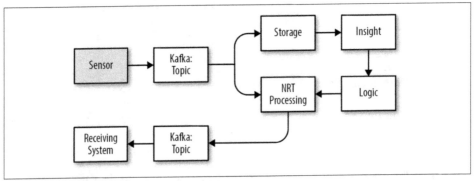

Figure 4-4. Data architecture compared to senses

Controllable systems

There are systems that can be controlled by communications sent through the PNS. Some of these systems are controlled through conscious thoughts and some via unconscious thoughts. These systems include muscles, heartbeats, and digestive functions.

In our data architecture, these are applications that process commands that are the outcome of data processing. A good example could be an application that customers interact with, and a command might be an instruction to lock down a person's account because of fraud risk. In our diagram, controllable systems are those that receive inputs from Kafka pipes, as shown in the highlighted box in Figure 4-5.

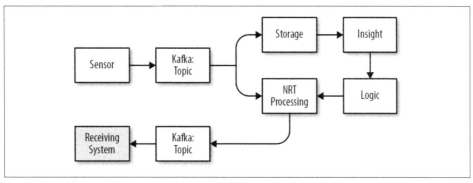

Figure 4-5. Data architecture compared to controllable systems

Human parts summary

Before we move on to more details of interface design, let's reflect for a minute on the body-part example. The main point to understand is that we have different components that make up a larger system. These systems collect data, store it, process it, or react to it. With all this communication, it's important that interfaces are clearly defined and agreed upon because the nature of these systems is that they are highly complex and operate independently. This means that they need to be *decoupled* in the correct ways. The same is true for complex data systems, so let's talk in more detail about decoupling.

Decoupling

Decoupling is a common architectural pattern in designing complex systems—this allows components in a system to be independent by taking advantage of interfaces between systems. To draw a parallel with the human body, let's consider the heart and the brain, as depicted in Figure 4-6. The brain is coupled (dependent) on the blood supplied by the heart, but not the heart itself. The heart could be replaced by a different "component"—for example, an artificial heart—without affecting the dependency that the brain has on blood flow. Thus the brain is coupled to the blood being pumped but not the system pumping the blood.

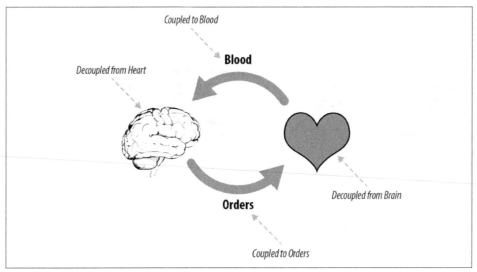

Figure 4-6. Decoupling in the human body

Decoupling applies itself throughout the human body, which is made up of trillions of cells and many subsystems. Subsystems in the body are commonly independent, with limited or no knowledge of the other components and how they work or what they are doing at any given moment; your heart knows nothing of your bladder, and your bladder is not concerned with the balancing sensors in the ear. The brain has a window of visibility into other systems but only through the messaging protocol that's supported by the PNS. Even your brain is made up of parts that are decoupled from one another, each having its own regions and responsibilities.

Modern medicine is able to increasingly use our biology to do things like bypass broken spinal cords or send messages straight from implanted chips in the brain to robotic limbs or even real limbs reanimated through controlled electric stimulation. Experiments have given blind people limited sight by having a camera send signals back into the brain through an embedded chip.

In the example of the blind person given sight via a camera, the brain doesn't know that the eyes have been replaced as the visual input system. The section of your brain that interprets visual information is interpreting the bits of information from the camera in a similar way as if it came from the eye.

In software architectures, this idea of decoupling systems through interface design is hugely important as a system grows and becomes increasingly complex. Good interface design will allow us to add, remove, and develop parts of our system without affecting the integrity of the system as a whole. When subsystems fail, we can bridge the gap and spin up new systems to replace them. And just like living organisms, decoupling in our architectures allows us to develop subsystems without disrupting the functioning of the entire system.

You can implement interface design in various ways: a distributed message system like Kafka, interfaces like Representational State Transfer (REST), public APIs, and message types like JSON, Avro, and Protobuffers.

To carry the parallels further, Kafka would be the transportation medium similar to the peripheral and central nervous systems, whereas JSON, Avro, and Protobuffers are the messages being sent through nerves. Figure 4-7 further illustrates this in a data system.

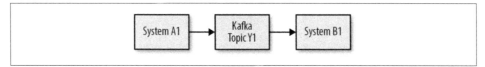

Figure 4-7. Decoupling with Kafka

Let's walk through a couple of decoupling options with this Kafka architecture:

Isolation
If system A stops working, it won't break system B. System B will just wait until A comes back online. Also, a failure in system B doesn't affect system A. This allows A and B to be tested independently from each other.

Replay
If we have a failure in system B, we can use the interface and ability to replay from Kafka to try to re-create the problem. This is important not only for testing for failure, but also for validation that newer versions of system B react to the data as the old versions did.

Extensible
This architecture allows us to add more systems that consume from topic Y1 without affecting system A1. This allows for architectures like that presented in Figure 4-8.

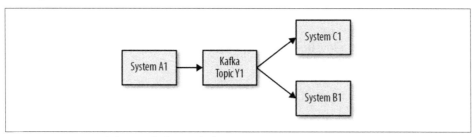

Figure 4-8. Extensibility with decoupled systems

Decoupling Considerations

As part of the work in creating artificial limbs, considerable research has gone into how the brain sends commands to other systems in the body; for example, instructing a hand to open or close. This process is illustrated in Figure 4-9. There was an idea before the research was done that maybe the brain sent detailed instructions to each muscle, but as scientists learned more, we now know that these commands sent from the brain are simply decoded near a specific system where more detailed actions are processed and executed. In the end, this process of sending messages to specific areas for decoding allows the brain to focus on more important things, whereas the individual systems can manage the details of executing commands. Over time these neural pathways can strengthen with repeated exposure to specific stimuli.

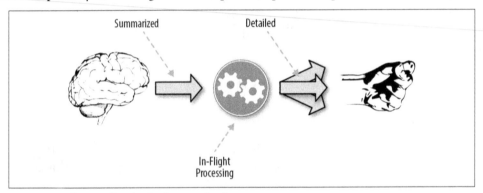

Figure 4-9. Decoupling in the human body

You can think of this concept as *muscle memory*. You will notice as you engage in repetitive actions such as sports or playing musical instruments that the practice leads to better performance and execution. Behind the scenes, you are optimizing operations and communications for certain instructions and building subroutines or models that execute the actions.

In the world of distributed data applications, we can see optimization and consolidation as the migration from ad hoc and batch processing to more real-time adaptive processing. Ad hoc and batch will always be present, but they should be there to get you closer to optimized processing. Just as with the body optimization allows you to do a task better, in the software architecture world, optimization can reduce SLAs, lead to better resource allocation, and facilitate more efficient processing. All of these can lead to better end-user experiences.

Specialization

The last area of the human body to consider is specialization. Consider the CNS and the brain specifically: the brain is made up of many subsystems, each with its unique region and responsibility. Some subsystems are for different types of storage, whereas some are for specific processing and access patterns.

Think about the storage systems in our brains. We have short-term memory, sensory memory, long-term memory, and implicit and explicit memory. Why so many memory types? The answer is there was an evolutionary benefit that each subsystem provided over having a generalized system. These various memory types most likely have different indexing strategies, flushing mechanisms, and aging-out/archiving processes. We find a parallel in software insomuch as we have different systems like relational databases, Lucene search engines, NoSQL stores, filesystems, block stores, distributed logs, and so forth that support different storage models and access patterns optimized for specific applications.

The same will go for our brain's processing systems. Visual interpretation is very different from complex decision making. Like the brain, in software architecture there are different execution patterns and optimizations that are suited for different use cases: tools like SQL, Spark, Spark SQL, NoSQL APIs, search queries, and many, many more.

What Makes a Good Interface Design

After that abstract discussion about how certain components in the human body parallel those in software architecture, let's examine what makes a good software interface design. You can consider interfaces to be the scaffolding of a large system—if you do it right, you can use your system for many years, changing it over time to meet the needs of many different use cases implemented by different technologies. If you do it wrong, it will be remembered as a poorly designed solution. Mastering interface design will be key to designing solid solutions.

The Contract

At the heart of a good interface definition is a contract between the implementers of the interface and the users of the interface. This contract must clearly define the inputs, outputs, and expected use and behavior of each function defined by the interface.

Whereas the functional specification is the core of an interface, secondary considerations are nonfunctional guarantees of the interface. In some cases we'll want to define secondary considerations like expected availability, response times, throughput, and so on—in other words, the SLAs provided by the interface. We discuss these considerations later in the chapter.

The Abstraction

When defining an interface, note that we are building an abstraction over our system —users of the interface shouldn't need to have visibility into the implementation of the system. This allows us to decouple our technology selections and concrete implementations from users of the system. Additionally, there are multiple options for how these interfaces are defined. Let's look at a couple of these options.

Nonprogramming language interface

The most common example of a higher-level, nonprogramming language interface is a REST interface. Generally speaking, REST is a stateless client–server interface that is built on common standards such as HTTP and JSON.

REST allows for a simple way to provide an interface to a backend service and allows for making calls to that service without writing code—calls to the REST API can be made via a web browser or command line. This makes it easy to test calls and create simple clients to the service. It also makes it easy to create client interfaces in common programming languages such as Java, Python, and C++ in order to facilitate programmatic access to a service.

Generally, the inputs and outputs of a REST command are JSON, which is human readable (although some might argue with this), great for exploratory work, and well supported by common programming languages.

Code interface implementations

Although REST is a common and effective way to implement interfaces in a system, sometimes there are advantages to a more direct client layer implemented via a programming API. Consider a Kafka producer, which might involve partitioning, buffering, batching, and complex protocols. Although there is a Kafka REST interface, the Kafka API provides a richer and more performant interface to Kafka.

You should aim for your interface to be common around all the implementations you support. In addition, openness is important. If you are building a piece of code that is planned to be deployed in a product that you don't own, it's important to allow that team to have access to details of your implementation. This doesn't necessarily need to be source code, but at a minimum this should include documentation, full interface definitions, and so on. In addition, by making the implementation open, you can get external help to flush out bugs, tune performance, and resolve issues.

Versioning

Versioning is important, particularly for interfaces heavily used by different applications. This includes backward compatibility. Note that backward compatibility is

---

painful, requiring additional testing and planning, but it is important. There are a few ways to help counter this pain:

- Make it easy to move to newer versions.

- Change the API as infrequently as possible.

- Be proactive about sharing information about deprecated calls and what's supported and not supported in specific releases.

- Strive to deliver regular release schedules. This will help your internal team determine when to deliver major functionality and facilitate the work of your interface's consumers by providing predictable updates.

A great example of versioning gone wrong, and then right, is Kafka. In versions of Kafka before 0.10, if producers or consumers were on a different version than the brokers, bad things could happen. With the release of 0.10, clients would tell the Kafka broker which version they were on, and the broker would use that protocol for communication.

Barring a complete migration on every API change (which is not realistic at scale), a strong versioning solution should be designed up front, starting with the aforementioned recommendations.

Being Defensive

Although we've emphasized the need to create stable, user-friendly interfaces, it's important to keep in mind that not all of the clients accessing your system are always friendly—either because of poorly implemented applications, maliciousness, or just problems in your design.

As a result, you must consider how others could use your interface to harm your system, and design safeguards for unexpected usage. Here are some common things to look for:

Skew
> If your system is a partitioned solution, skew can cause untold trouble for you— this is the case in which some partitions become much larger than other partitions. Look for skew and stop it before it causes disaster. Note that data skew is a potential problem that goes beyond the scope of this discussion, but it is still something to be mindful of when designing your interfaces.

Load
> A Denial-of-Service (DoS) attack, either inadvertent or malicious, can be disastrous for your system. Set up ways to look for load spikes and handle them.

Odd input

If you make an input a string, assume that *anything* will be passed through. Think about past issues with SQL injection, or null values, or extremely large values. Make sure you validate all inputs to the system.

Documentation and Naming for Interfaces

Ideally, documentation for APIs is brief and to the point—good documentation should be concise and direct. If it takes a book to define your API, that could be a sign that your API is too complex. It should be the goal of any API or interface designer to create an interface so clear that documentation becomes unnecessary.

The documentation should focus on how this interface will behave, how to use the interface, and examples of use.

Important things to note in your documentation include the following:

- What calls (functions) are provided by the interface.
- Arguments to the calls defined by the interface, including formats, schemas, data types, and so on.
- Outputs from calls, including detail on formats, schemas, data types, and so forth.
- State requirements; for example, does the service maintain state or is this expected to be a stateless service?
- Support and behavior in concurrent scenarios; for example, support for multiple requests.
- Known failure cases/possible exceptions.

Similarly, naming of functions should be simple and explanatory. Ideally, the purpose of the function should be clear from the name and parameters.

Try to avoid putting technology solutions in the function name or definition. Think more of the function as being a verb. Let's take a real-world example and relate that to our computer-world example.

Our example function will be the call `goToLocation(locationId:String)`. In the real world, if we called `goToLocation("Market")`, we could implement this with walking, driving, bicycling, and so on. However, we don't put any of that in the function name. All that the function and the users using the function need to know is the action (verb) the function is performing.

There's a joke that naming is one of the most difficult things to do in software development. The best rule of thumb that we have found to reduce the time naming takes is to copy the style of a respected project in the same ecosystem. This provides two advantages:

- It provides a guideline to follow.
- It provides an external objective reference to back up your decisions.

In the end, know that no matter how hard you try to design something, you will look back on it in a year or two and see things you wished you'd done better. It is just the nature of our world. Aiming for simple and repeatable is most likely your best bet.

Nonfunctional Considerations

As noted in the previous section, there are secondary, nonfunctional considerations to take into account when designing your interface. These include things like guarantees around availability of the system, response times of the system, and throughput. We'll explore these considerations in this section.

Availability

All interfaces will specify a functional contract, but interfaces that define access to services or that interact with an external system might also need to specify the availability contracts. If the interface is defining the contract for a library that's loaded locally to a program, defining availability would be irrelevant. However, if the interface is for an external service, providing a clear contract for when the service is available and the level of guarantee for service availability becomes much more important.

Think of this as the hours of business for a given service and the level of guarantee a customer has to which those hours are going to be committed. In a real-world example, we can compare the hours of a supermarket and a movie theater. Both will have hours of operation: suppose for the supermarket it is 6:00 A.M. to 10:00 P.M., and the movie theater is 10:00 A.M. to midnight.

Given these stated hours, we have some level of knowledge of which hours the supermarket and the movie theater will be open. However, things can happen that disrupt these expected hours; for example, during a heavy snowstorm the movie theater might shut down, whereas the supermarket remains open. In these cases, we can reasonably have an expectation that the supermarket holds itself to a higher guarantee level than the movie theater.

So, the takeaway here is that we need to provide two definitions of availability: the first is when the service will be available, and the second is the level of guarantee for those availability times.

You might be saying, "In the computer world, shouldn't my services always be available?" Let's look at examples of different availability levels:

Scheduled maintenance windows
> It's common for a service to have a scheduled period during which the service is unavailable in order to allow for maintenance tasks to the service such as performing software upgrades, applying patches, and swapping out hardware.

Only during specific hours
> Some services may need to be available only within certain defined hours; for example, a service that's expected to be accessed only during business hours. With the introduction of the cloud and the ability to start and stop services with a push of a button, it becomes practical (and economical) to provide availability for services only during these limited hours.

In addition to these expected availability windows, numerous things can disrupt availability such as hardware failures, network failures, and cloud outages. For these reasons, it's impossible to promise 100% uptime during the documented availability windows, although there are ways to increase the level of confidence in the uptime percentage, including the following:

- Utilizing components that are resilient to failure. Most of the systems discussed throughout this book as components in a big data application are designed for high availability and resistance to failure. For example, Kafka provides a data integration solution that's designed to be scalable, replicated, and highly available. When deployed properly, Kafka provides a very resilient data integration layer. Similarly, other systems in the big data ecosystem can provide these types of resilience in other layers of our architectures, such as storage and processing.

- Building redundancy into the system. Even the most resilient distributed system can fail, which is why having backup systems becomes crucial in mission-critical systems. This is a complex topic, and the mechanism to achieve redundancy will vary with different systems. Refer to vendor or project documentation for recommendations and details on how to deploy those systems in order to ensure you have the necessary levels of availability.

- Using testing, including load testing and failure testing. We discuss this more in the section "Using Testing to Determine SLAs" on page 81.

Response-Time Guarantees

Like availability, response times are never perfect. Things like system failures, garbage collection, network latency, and more can affect response times of a service.

We should aim to give our users a tested and confirmed set of guarantees based on percentage of time; for example:

- Response times of 10 milliseconds 95% of the time
- Response times of 50 milliseconds 99% of the time
- Response times of 1,000 milliseconds 99.99% of the time

Note that an advantage of using interfaces is that you can enhance the availability and response times of an implementation over time without disrupting clients using the system. It's critical, though, that you have a testing framework in place to perform load testing of the system with every release to ensure adherence to your contracts.

Load Capacity

Load capacity defines how many requests can be handled in a given time period, and the limitations to scaling. Again, we don't talk about how we provide these load guarantees in our contract; instead, we include a promise of what level of load capacity we will be offering. Just like availability and response time, we need to give detailed promises to our interface users. Here's an example:

When under 100,000 requests a second:

- Response times of 10 milliseconds 95% of the time
- Response times of 50 milliseconds 99% of the time
- Response times of 1,000 milliseconds 99.99% of the time

When between 100,000 and 200,000 requests a second:

- Response times of 20 milliseconds 95% of the time
- Response times of 100 milliseconds 99% of the time
- Response times of 2,000 milliseconds 99.99% of the time
- Not recommended beyond 200,000 requests a second

It's recommended to keep these load definitions simple and, as appropriate, call out any specific limitations. As with availability and response times, you'll have to load test on every release at a minimum and closely monitor activity in your production systems.

Using Testing to Determine SLAs

Regardless of your architecture and component selection, the only way to truly determine the guarantees that you can make around availability and response times is to test the system. You need to do this testing in the target deployment environment, using real-world data and under expected loads.

For example, if you claim in your interface that your system is safe from node failure, you should test random node failures on a regular basis in both your test and production systems. This type of testing in production might raise concerns—if so, this might reflect a lack of confidence in your system's ability to recover, and in turn indicates a need to put more thought into your system's failure recovery capabilities.

Without testing and simulating failure in a system, you know only in theory how it will handle failures. If your system is said to handle a node failure, no one should be paged at 3 A.M. when a node fails. Such failures need to be an expected occurrence, with self-healing mechanisms.

Common Interface Examples

Now that we have covered what makes a good interface design, let's look at some common architectural patterns that are used in creating system interfaces.

Publish–Subscribe

The first pattern we'll talk about is the common publish–subscribe (pub–sub) example, shown in Figure 4-10. In this implementation, we have components that publish messages to a central messaging system (broker), and components that subscribe to specific queues on the broker.

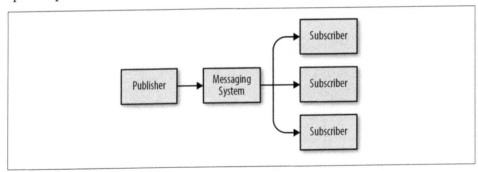

Figure 4-10. Pub–sub system

The central idea here is that the publisher on the left side need not care about anything going on with the subscribers on the right side. Publishers need to worry only about sending messages with content that matches what's defined by the interface. These publishers don't care who reads the messages or what those readers do with the messages.

In the context of application development, the pub–sub pattern allows components to be developed in isolation. Consider Figure 4-11. In this case, development on the subscribers is complete, but work on the publisher is still in progress. In this case, you can create a mock publisher, which allows development and testing to continue, avoiding disruption to the development schedule.

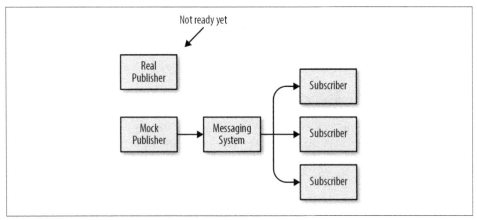

Figure 4-11. Decoupling with pub–sub systems

Enterprise Service Bus

Somewhat similar to the pub–sub model, but generally at a larger scale, is an Enterprise Service Bus (ESB) architecture. An ESB architecture will most likely have the following features:

Transport layer
There is a requirement for a reliable, scalable pipe to accept messages and deliver them to one or more destination(s).

Publishers
There are a number of systems that publish events to a network of topics on the message bus.

Consumers
There are systems that listen to and consume messages.

Workflow
There could be systems with workflow logic that can take an event and update state or determine what additional actions need to happen or whether additional events need to be fired.

Asynchronous requests
There could also be a good deal of asynchronous request patterns used. We look at that pattern in the next subsection.

Dashboards
> There most likely is a dashboarding system that is in place that can monitor the state of the ESB and the state of all systems publishing to it.

ESBs were popular for a time in the earlier 2000s. However, there were issues around scale and coordination within an organization. It wasn't until the success of Kafka and a centralized schema repository that the ESB concept made a comeback.

Request–Response Asynchronous Example

We've discussed the pub–sub model, which is a one-way interface, but what if we need to give responses back to requests? This will be the first example of a request–response interface, in this case an asynchronous model, versus a synchronous model that is discussed in the next section.

Before we begin looking at the example, let's consider when an asynchronous request–response model is something we want to consider:

- We want to request some information from a component.
- We don't have hard latency requirements on when the response should be returned to us.
- Duplicate responses are acceptable.
- We're aware of resource requirements for this architecture; for example, memory requirements to persist maps of requests and message queues.

If this is a fit for your use case, an example architecture might look like that shown in Figure 4-12.

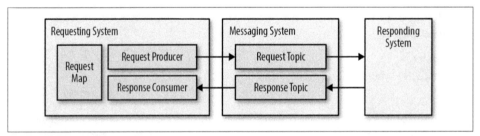

Figure 4-12. Asynchronous request–response architecture

Let's look at some of the components in the diagram:

Requesting system
> This is simply the system that is making requests.

Request map

This is a data structure that maintains the list of requests that have been submitted and are awaiting a response. The request map will consume memory for every outstanding request, which means that there's a limit to the number of outstanding requests that can be stored based on memory constraints.

Request producer

This is the component that sends requests along with a key (for use in indexing the request map) to the messaging system.

Request topic

This is a dedicated queue for the requests being sent out. This topic can be shared with other requests, but note that it would be wise to balance the use of this topic with throughput and response times. Also, any request in this topic should be going to the same responding system.

Responding system

This is a system that takes a given request and returns an answer. Ideally, this system has no state itself but can work with stateful systems.

Response topic

This is the queue for response messages. The important thing to note is the number of requesting systems assigned to a given response topic. The more requesting systems assigned to a given response topic, the more responses will have to be dropped by a specific requesting system because it doesn't need the responses intended for other requesting systems.

Response consumer

This is the consumer that is listening to the response topic and will be using the request map to link responses back to the original thread that requested the information. If the request is not in the request map, that response has already been processed or the response was meant for another requesting system but used the same response topic.

The big advantage with this type of interface design is that it allows us to decouple the processing of the request from the response and gives the responder flexibility in terms of time constraints to return results back to the requester.

This is normally a good solution for requests that take a long time (many seconds to hours) to process. However, this doesn't mean that you can't use it for more real-time solutions. Suppose that you use Kafka as the queue along with some basic processing before returning a response. In this case, you could be looking at a couple to tens of milliseconds of latency round-trip, depending on the system being queried.

Request–Response Synchronous Example

The last interface design we explore is a request–response interaction that is synchronous and has a tight SLA for response times. In this model, we don't need any queues; instead, we need only old-fashioned web servers. In this model, shown in Figure 4-13, we have the requesting system that sends a request and then simply waits for the answering system to return a reply. As you can see, this request and response happens in a single transaction, which can provide advantages in terms of response guarantees, reduction of latency, and removing the need to consider the possibility of duplicate responses.

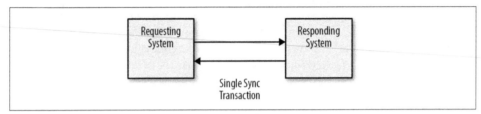

Figure 4-13. Synchronous request–response architecture

This can present challenges in terms of scaling because network bandwidth, hardware resources, and so on could affect response times and the number of requests that can be processed. This also presents challenges for the cases in which the answering system is unavailable. If we are worried about web servers going down or load, we can support multiple systems that are behind a load balancer with a virtual IP address, as shown in Figure 4-14. This is basically the architecture that supports many web applications.

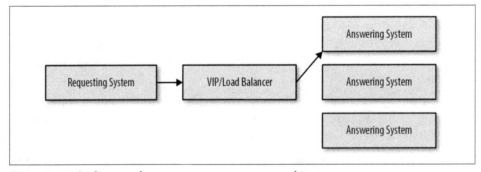

Figure 4-14. Scaling synchronous request–response architectures

Summary

Just like the human body, scalable and maintainable software architectures rely on interfaces and abstractions. Well-designed abstractions allow us to decouple concrete implementation decisions from overall architectures. This decoupling facilitates the development process by allowing us to create mock implementations of services and shields us from implementation changes within systems.

There are a number of ways in which we can implement our interfaces, such as standard APIs, REST interfaces, and publish–subscribe systems. The choice of how to design your interface should be influenced by your architecture and requirements; for example, if your system is a straightforward Java application, defining Java APIs might be sufficient. Alternatively, if you need to allow for access from multiple languages or external hosts, a REST interface becomes a more likely solution.

In addition to the functional interface design, you also need to be mindful of nonfunctional requirements. These considerations include defining the availability of services that implement the interface, and response times and throughput for the services.

Finally, there are several architectural models to consider when creating system interfaces, including publish–subscribe systems, and synchronous and asynchronous request–response systems.

CHAPTER 5

Distributed Storage Systems

After talking about interface design in Chapter 4, we're going to move on to discuss the available distributed storage systems that you're likely to consider for your data architectures. As we discuss the variety of storage systems available, hopefully it will become apparent why interfaces are so useful when designing data applications.

In this chapter, we first discuss some core attributes of a distributed storage system to categorize the options. Then, we dig into some of the currently available and widely used distributed storage systems. We start with a discussion of these attributes because it would be impossible for this book to cover all the storage systems out there, and by the time this book comes out, there will likely be more. Fortunately, with a strong understanding of the fundamentals of distributed storage systems, you should be able to categorize and evaluate any new systems that come along.

Attributes of Distributed Storage Systems

People categorize distributed storage systems in numerous ways—some being helpful and some being confusing. The goal of this section is to call out what we consider to be important when evaluating storage systems for your data applications.

Note that the considerations for evaluating systems discussed in Chapter 2 are relevant to evaluating the systems discussed here. We're not going to reiterate those considerations, but it will be helpful to keep them in mind as you read this chapter.

We begin by talking about the historical origins of the major distributed storage systems currently available (spoiler alert: most of them are descended from Google projects). We then go on to talk about the following criteria that you can use to evaluate and categorize systems:

Partitioning
> How does the system manage distribution of data across nodes?

Mutation
> What support does the system have for modifying data?

Read paths
> How is data in the system accessed?

Availability and consistency
> What trade-offs does the system make in terms of availability of the system versus consistency of data?

Use cases
> Finally, to what problems does a system provide a solution?

Storage System Genealogy

Genealogy isn't necessarily something you'd expect in a discussion of storage systems, but consider that a distributed storage system is highly complex, and is usually built based on design principles from existing systems. As we already gave away, most of the systems discussed here have roots in Google projects like Google File System (GFS), BigTable, Spanner, and Google Search.

As a specific example, Cassandra and HBase are both based on BigTable. Knowing this genealogy tells you a lot about these systems, such as the following:

- Components of their architecture are similar.
- They are key–value stores.
- They are designed to scale well.
- They enforce ordering as part of how they store data on disk and index it.
- Under the hood, data is immutable, but there are patterns that allow data to be mutable.
- They aim to solve similar use cases (for example, fast point access to records) and have similar performance characteristics.

The image in Figure 5-1 is a high-level genealogy diagram of some current distributed data stores. It's likely that some of the connections here will be controversial, but this group is a good place to begin nonetheless. Also note that connections don't indicate a project is an extension of a project above it; rather, it indicates that parent projects had a significant impact on the project.

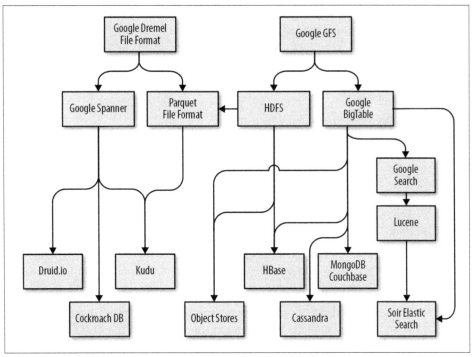

Figure 5-1. Distributed storage system genealogy

There are a few ways these projects can be seen as connected:

Direct descendent from Google

An example is the connection from Google File System (GFS) to Hadoop Distributed File System (HDFS). This is a case in which the open source community created a project based on a closed-source Google solution.

Inspired lineage

An example is the connection from Parquet to Kudu. One of the initial ideas for Kudu came from the advantages of the Parquet columnar file type, including greater compression and faster read times.

Addressing gaps

A good example of this is the lineage from HDFS to object stores. In general, HDFS is a poor object store, which leads to data stores that provide better support for object storage.

Partitioning

Distributed storage systems scale because they use *partitioning* of information—in this case, partitioning refers to how the system determines which nodes store data; in other words, the mechanism used to distribute data across the system. In general, a limited number of options for data partitioning exist in distributed storage systems: *centralized*, *range*, and *hash partitioning*. The following subsections address each one of these partitioning types.

Centralized partitioning

Utilized in storage systems such as GFS and HDFS, centralized partitioning relies on a single service that determines which nodes data will live on. Although this model provides advantages, there are also drawbacks that are leading to less usage of this model.

The advantage of this type of system is that the centralized node can make sure the data is partitioned evenly, even in the cases of data node failure. The central service knows where everything is and can point to it at any time.

Drawbacks to this system include the potential bottleneck created by having one metadata service because it will be constrained in terms of memory and in terms of throughput for requests in multitenant environments.

In addition, a centralized partitioning system will use an algorithm to place data on nodes based on the current state of the system. As we go into the other partitioning options, you will notice no other partitioning solution will use existing state as a factor for a partition decision. This is because it's costly to know the state of a large distributed system, and this cost can affect performance and scalability.

Range partitioning

Range partitioning is another common mechanism that is used in systems like HBase and Cassandra. However, Cassandra adds a hash to the key by default (we talk about hashing in the next subsection).

A good real-world example of range partitioning is a dictionary (you know, the old-fashioned hard-copy kind). In a dictionary there are range partitions for each letter in the alphabet. Just from glancing at a dictionary, you should be able to see there is a fundamental problem with a range partitioning strategy—that problem is known as *skew*.

Skew occurs when one partition has a significantly larger amount of content versus the other partitions. In our dictionary example, we can see that the letters S and T have far more words than X and Z. This isn't too bad for a dictionary, but for a distributed system this will result in some nodes doing more work than other nodes, which is not a good option. So, let's solve this. To do that, we apply *hashing*, as discussed in the next section.

Hash partitioning

In the computer science world, a hash function is a way to convert a given value into a more limited range. For example, if I use Java and get the hash of the string "ted" and "jon," I will get 114707 and 105417, respectively. Let's walk through how this seemingly random repeatable number can help us put different records into partitions:

```
val recordKey = "ted"

val hashCode = recordKey.hashCode
//hashCode = 114707

val absHash = Math.abs(hashCode)
//We need to use absolute value because the hash may be negative
//absHash = 114707

val numOfPartitions = 10
//number of partitions will be defined on how you set up your table

//Find the modulus of the hash and the number of partitions
val destinationPartition = absHash % numOfPartitions
//destinationPartition = 7
```

So how does this apply to our skew problem? An effective hash function (and smart use of hash keys) can evenly spread data values across partitions, ensuring that data is evenly distributed across our cluster.

Some systems such as Cassandra or Elasticsearch use hash partitioning, but in general a system that uses range partitioning can use hash partitioning by prepending a hash to the keys used by the system.

Mutation Options

After partitioning strategies, the next big consideration of a distributed storage system to consider is how the system handles mutations. When we refer to mutations, we're really just talking about how the system handles modifications to records stored in the system. Common distributed storage systems are highly tuned for specific types of data and access patterns and have different ways of handling mutations. Let's dig into these different types of mutation patterns that we see in storage systems.

Append only

Some storage systems allow data to only be appended, in the same way that you append lines to a log or add a new file to a folder. You can't change values in those logs or files after they have been written. A specific example is HDFS, in which you can delete the file and rewrite it, but you can't change it.

You might ask why build a storage system that's append only? Because mutation in place is not easy. You either need very fixed data structures that might not compress well or you have blocks of data that you have to rewrite. So, when it comes to storing large volumes and varieties of data, those fixed data structures would be wasteful. Additionally, rewriting large datasets would also be too expensive for a low-latency storage system. A better answer, which we talk about later, is an approach called append and compact. It is the style all NoSQL systems use to simulate mutation while using immutable files.

File versus record

Another consideration is the level at which mutation takes place—file or record. As you might guess, in a file-based system or object store, mutation takes place at the file level, whereas with other stores such as a NoSQL-type system, mutations are record or document based.

The level at which mutation occurs will generally inform us as to the default level of transactions in a system. For example, in a filesystem or object store, transactions will be at the file/object level, whereas in a NoSQL-type system, the transaction level will probably be at the record level.

Record size

The next mutation factor to consider is the optimal size of records for specific storage systems. Some systems, like object stores and HDFS, are optimized for larger chunks of data where file sizes of 100 MB into the gigabyte range are good. However, other systems work better with data chunks under or around 10 KB; for example, HBase and Cassandra.

These size preferences are all about how the system stores and mutates the data on disk. It's important to be mindful of these recommendations for you to make optimal use of the system. Using the wrong file or record size with a storage system might cause problems—for example, using an object store such as Amazon Web Services Simple Storage Service (Amazon S3) with a large number of small files.

An object store, unlike HDFS, doesn't have limitations that come with centralized management of metadata (more about this later), So it is well suited to be able to handle the storage of a lot of small files. This, however, can cause other problems. Suppose that we store 10 GB of data in 1 KB files. That will give us about 10 million files. Then, we run a Hive job on that folder or table. What we will get is a long wait followed by an out-of-memory exception. The reason is that Hive (and most execution systems) needs to build an execution plan. That execution plan needs to determine which files it should be reading in to execute the query, and 10 million files is outside the default memory setting for Hive.

In general, this 10 GB example would have given better execution performance with file sizes of 100 MB to 250 MB. Additionally, because there is more data in each file, there is a good chance that it will provide better compression ratios because of the greater likelihood of repeated data patterns. Another potential consideration is that the number of file handlers required to process a large number of files can have performance implications.

So, the takeaway is that even if your file or object store doesn't have a small-file problem, you should still aim for files around 100 MB or over.

Mutation latency

Different storage systems are optimized for reading and writing different batch sizes with different transaction boundaries. For example, NoSQL stores like HBase and Cassandra can operate at millisecond levels of batches; in other words, these systems are able to process batches of records arriving within millisecond frequency. Lucene-based systems such as Solr are tuned to process record batches spanning seconds to minutes, and HDFS is designed for record batches on the order of minutes.

Read Paths

In the old days, when we had single-node relational databases, the read path was easy. But now that data is too large to fit in the memory of a single node and is therefore spread across many nodes, different systems have different methods to access data. Following are methods that distributed storage systems will use to access data.

Indexing

Indexing is widely used in distributed systems but often in different ways. Some systems will index only the start of a file, leaving all the content in that file for a scan to filter through. Other systems will index every field in a record and even content within a record.

In general, there are four categories of indexing in distributed systems:

Indexing at the file level
  One index for chunks of data.

Indexing at the record level
  Every record or document has a primary key and is indexed by that value.

Simple secondary indexing
  Simple secondary indexes on fields that are not the primary key.

Reverse indexing
  Lucene-based indexing (see the following sidebar) in which everything can be indexed. This is used mainly for searching or faceting use cases.

Lucene-Based Reverse Indexing

If you're already familiar with systems like Lucene and solutions that build on Lucene such as Solr and Elasticsearch, you can skip this section. Otherwise, let's dig a little deeper into how reverse indexing works. Figure 5-2 shows an example of reverse indexing on the field color and size.

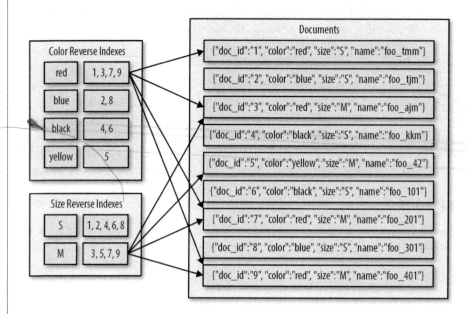

Figure 5-2. Reverse indexing example

The big difference from a standard indexing scheme is that we don't use the doc_id to get to the record; instead, we can use "black" to find that there are two records that have the color field as black.

This is powerful for searching, but it is also powerful for making charts and graphs based on counts on different field values. For example, if we wanted to make a count of documents with red, blue, black, and yellow, all we would need to do is count the number of doc_id's in the *Color Reverse Indexes*. So, we can produce a chart without even having to read the original data.

Also, if we wanted to make a chart based on colors and size, we can even do a merge join to get the combined charts. Figure 5-3 shows how a join between red and M would happen. Note that because the data is already ordered, we just join as we scan over the doc_ids.

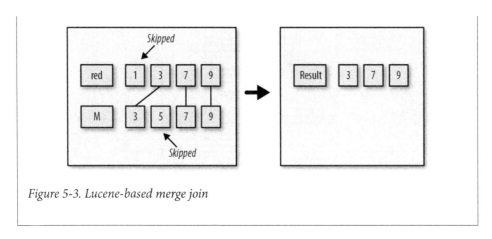

Figure 5-3. Lucene-based merge join

Row-based versus columnar storage

The term "columnar" can be confusing because some distributed stores are referred to as "column-oriented"—for example, HBase. In the context of this section, when we talk about columnar storage versus row-based storage formats, we're referring to the format used to store datasets in persistent storage. To help clarify this, let's consider a typical dataset containing multiple records, in which each record contains a fixed set of columns, and each column is assigned a specific data type. Figure 5-4 provides an illustration of our example dataset containing rows and columns.

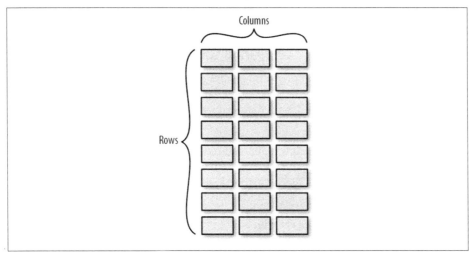

Figure 5-4. Row versus columnar storage

A row-based system will store and compress the data into groups of rows, as demonstrated in Figure 5-5.

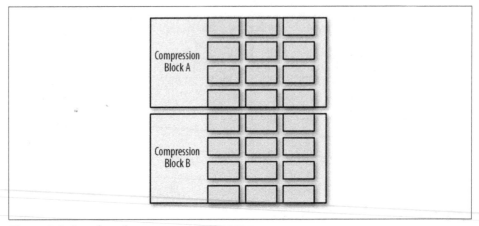

Figure 5-5. Row-based storage

In a row-based system, you will note that all the cells of different columns are stored next to one another. With this approach, we can reduce the amount of memory needed when writing out to disk as well as reading from disk. On the other hand, when writing to files within a columnar storage system, a memory buffer is required for every column for writing and reading. So, in general the files used with row-based storage systems are more efficient and faster when writing and reading. However, comparing speed depends on a great number of details. The sidebar that follows provides an explanation.

Comparing Speed

At this point in the chapter, determining whether row-based formats will be faster than columnar formats is a difficult question. Let's point out why row-based formats are not always faster, even though they require a good deal less effort to read from:

Compression
Row-based formats generally don't compress as efficiently as columnar-based formats, so in some cases the throughput is a limiting factor (for example, when using Amazon S3 for storage).

Code paths
Even if the code path is easier with a row-based format, columnar-based storage formats like Parquet and ORC have been tuned very heavily over the years. So, even if they are doing more work, they still might be faster because they are optimized better.

As always, benchmark with your data and your storage system.

There are two downsides to the row-based model. The first issue is compression ratios, because cells grouped by different columns will generally have different data types, which doesn't facilitate compression—grouping like values together is better for compression. For example, consider a table containing stock ticker records comprising three columns: ticker, time, price. The time values are more like other time values than they are like ticker values. The second problem occurs when you want to read only a subset of the values, which of course is a common query pattern. In the row-based model, you still need to read all the columns even if you want only a subset.

The columnar storage format, illustrated in Figure 5-6, helps address these problems. In this case, we're storing columns together rather than rows, which allows for better compression of data as well as faster read times for queries selecting a subset of values.

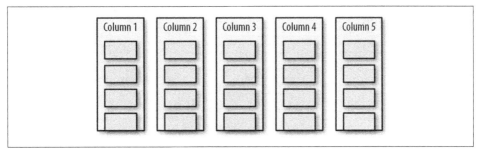

Figure 5-6. Columnar-based storage

Partitioning

Partitioning is definitely an overloaded term in this discussion. In this context, we're talking about partitioning in the sense of storing data based on one or more data fields that act as a key. This is supported by systems like Apache Hive, which allows data partitions to be defined at the table level based on specific table columns. This partitioning can help improve the efficiency of access by allowing irrelevant records to be pruned during queries. For example, if records are partitioned by years, queries for specific years can just ignore partitions for years that are not part of the query.

Availability Versus Consistency

Distributed systems inevitably fail, but the characteristics of specific systems will affect the failure behavior of those systems. This means that we need to discuss what we have to give up when failure occurs, depending on which particular storage system we choose. Before we discuss the specifics of these trade-offs, let's briefly talk about the CAP theorem.

The CAP theorem

Per Wikipedia (*https://en.wikipedia.org/wiki/CAP_theorem*), the CAP theorem "states that it is impossible for a distributed data store to simultaneously provide more than two out of the following three guarantees:

- Consistency guarantee: Every read should receive the most current version of data.

- Availability: Every read receives a valid response although without a guarantee that it's the most current version of the data.

- Partition tolerance: The system continues to function despite message loss between nodes."

Because network failure is inevitable in a distributed system, we already know that we need to tolerate network partitioning, which means the decision comes down to consistency versus availability, as shown in Figure 5-7.

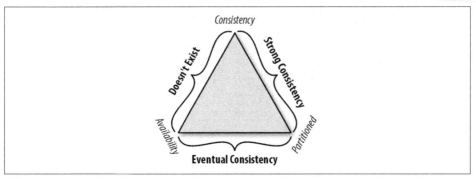

Figure 5-7. Consistency versus availability

Choosing availability: eventual consistency

Eventual consistency is a model in which all requests for data will eventually return the same value. This model gives up data consistency for greater availability. When we give up consistency in favor of availability, in the event of system failure there might be some cases in which we lose data, but, more important, we are not guaranteed to get the most up-to-date data when requesting a value.

Choosing consistency: strongly consistent

Strong consistency, as the name suggests, guarantees that accesses to specific data return the same value. So, if we give up availability in favor of consistency, if failure occurs, we lose the ability to read and write to a partition of the system for a given amount of time.

In general, the choice between consistency and availability will be determined by your use case. However, the choice of storage system will sometimes dictate the model; for example, HBase favors consistency over availability. Cassandra, on the other hand, favors availability over consistency, although, as we note shortly, Cassandra provides some control over consistency models.

Primary Use Cases

The last consideration that we should call out for our storage systems is the primary usage pattern for which they were designed to handle. Note that we can use a system to handle more than one use case, but some systems are highly tuned for a narrow set of usage patterns and will fail if used with the wrong goals in mind. As we go through the different use cases, we'll note which systems are generally a fit for each case and then provide more context in the detailed discussion of each system.

Large scans

This is the case in which you want to do large scans over your data, for example partitioning the data by date or some other large partition boundary, but nothing smaller than a million records in a partition. The main use cases here are things like queries that access large blocks of records, machine learning, graph processing, and windowing operations. For these use cases, we'll generally be looking at file-based storage systems like HDFS or an object store.

Random access to data

Rather than scans of large blocks of data, now we want to quickly access one or more records, or update a record within a millisecond or so. For this, we need a highly mutable and indexed system. NoSQL systems like HBase or Cassandra will generally be the best fit for use cases requiring this type of access.

Cubing

In this use case, we are aiming to do a lot of analyses and deep drills. In this model, we need our data to be highly optimized for querying from many different angles. This use case is where Lucene-based systems such as Elasticsearch and Solr can provide a solution.

Time series

In applications such as the Internet of Things (IoT), we need to be able to store and access a large number of events with respect to time. For this, we need a storage system that is optimized for ordering. For these types of applications, a NoSQL system like HBase can provide a solution as well as data stores like Druid.

High mutability

There are some use cases that we will dive into, like sorted lists or streaming windows, that require mutation of state at a very high rate. These will tend to be more in-memory systems such as Druid or Redis designed for a given type of mutation to be optimized.

Storage System Breakdown

At this point, we have gone over the following:

Genealogy
Knowing a system's origins

Partitioning
Knowing a system's strategy for placing data on different nodes

Mutation options
Knowing a system's write behavior and how data modification is handled

Optimal read paths
Knowing a system's data access behavior

Availability versus consistency
Knowing whether the system favors availability of data or consistency of data

Primary use case
Knowing what the system was designed for

Now we are going to look at some of the most popular of the currently available open source distributed storage solutions in the context of these considerations.

HDFS

We begin our survey of distributed storage systems by looking at how HDFS fits into our set of characteristics for storage systems.

Genealogy

HDFS, part of the Apache Hadoop project, is an open source project that was started in the mid 2000s with early support from Yahoo!. HDFS is essentially an open source port of the GFS.

The initial application of Hadoop was to develop an internet reverse-indexing framework to support search for Yahoo!. This application required storing an extremely large volume of data and efficiently running distributed processing of the data via Hadoop MapReduce.

Partitioning

In HDFS, we have a name node that holds the metadata for all the data block locations in the cluster. The name node is responsible for designating block node assignments, fetching block node assignments, and handling rebalancing operations.

With respect to the partitioning patterns, HDFS falls under the centralized partitioning mechanism, with all its pluses and minuses.

Mutation Options

Files in HDFS are append only; you can append to a file until it is closed. After it is closed, the file is immutable. If you need to change information within HDFS, you need to rewrite the file. Generally, a pattern known as *compaction* is used when rewriting files to mutate records. Figure 5-8 gives us some insight into what a compaction looks like.

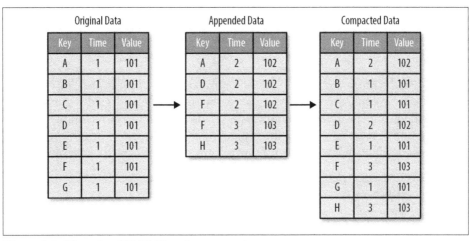

Figure 5-8. Changing HDFS files via compaction

We see this pattern in almost all of the following systems that allow mutations, but unlike most of those systems, with HDFS you need to do this manually—systems like Cassandra, HBase, Solr, and others will do this compaction behind the scenes. However, unlike the other systems, which are optimized for edits, HDFS will not be able to show the new mutated records until the file rewriting is fully done.

Optimal read path

For the most part, HDFS is designed for scans of large blocks of data. However, there has been investment in advanced file formats like Parquet and Optimized Row Columnar (ORC) that allow users to avoid reading rows and columns based on push-down filters. Random access to records is not really possible, and support for indexing is extremely limited.

Primary use case

If you are storing a lot of data (terabytes to petabytes or more) on premises and you want to do queries or processing that need access to large blocks of data, such as machine learning or Extract, Transform, and Load (ETL), HDFS is an option for you.

Additionally, with HDFS being in the datacenter, it was normal to have the storage node also have compute attached. For a long time, it was promoted that HDFS allowed you to move your execution closer to your data by processing data on the nodes where it was stored.

S3 and Object Stores

We now move on to look at how object stores such as Amazon S3 fit into our storage system taxonomy.

Genealogy

With HDFS, the focus was on data locality. However, the advent of the cloud ushered in a move away from data locality, primarily because the cloud made it practical to pay for storage independent from processing. This allowed for many options to optimize cost and resources, whereas the Hadoop and HDFS model encouraged colocated processing and storage. Figure 5-9 shows some options enabled by the cloud.

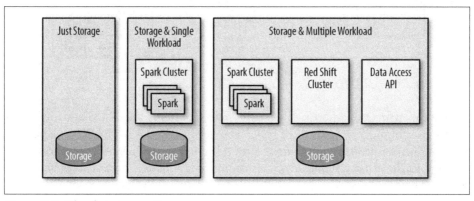

Figure 5-9. Cloud storage options

As this push from locality to nonlocality in the cloud happened, it brought about the rise of the *object store*. Amazon's S3 is the current predominant example, although all of the major cloud vendors have their own object stores such as Microsoft's Azure Blob Store or the Google Cloud Store. Even on-premises cloud solutions have object stores, with Swift being a prime example.

Object stores in general give up locality and fast metadata scan rates and have an eventually consistent model for metadata. Note that we're talking about the consistency model for metadata, and not the actual data in this context. To make this more concrete, with HDFS, placement of data blocks in a cluster is centralized within the NameNode component of the HDFS architecture. The NameNode will record the locations of each data block after writing all blocks.

In contrast, with an object store such as S3, it's possible that listing objects in a bucket might not return correct results immediately after writing data or removing data in some cases. Although there are drawbacks to the S3 model, removing the centralized partitioning scheme followed by a system like HDFS provides the scale required for a modern cloud data store.

Partitioning

Specific implementations vary, but all object stores utilize some form of hash partitioning for distribution of data.

Mutation options

Like HDFS, object stores write in units of files or blobs. And just like HDFS, these files or objects are append only and immutable after they are created. Also, similarly, all the write patterns, file types, and directory patterns still apply to object stores. You can even run Hive on an object store and make tables on top of the files and folders.

The main difference from a system like HDFS is that there is a higher importance on compressing your data in an object store. There are two reasons for this: first to reduce your long-term storage cost, and second because you want to limit network usage as the data is transferred to the compute nodes for processing.

Optimal read path

As with any distributed storage system, data is traveling over the network, so compress and cache when needed. As we discussed earlier, a major difference between an object store and a system like HDFS is metadata management. On the plus side, you no longer have the single NameNode bottleneck as with HDFS. The negative is that your metadata is eventually consistent so it might be out-of-date, and retrieving file and directory lists is not as efficient.

Primary use case

If you're running in the cloud, an object store will be your primary long-term data store, acting as a replacement for systems like HDFS. Even if you are not storing your data in the cloud, you might want to look at technology like OpenStack's Swift for object storage within your datacenter.

Apache HBase

After discussing file- and object-based stores such as HDFS and S3, let's move on to discuss storage systems designed for specific access patterns, starting with HBase.

Genealogy

In 2006, Google released a whitepaper on BigTable, a NoSQL store that ran on the GFS. HBase was one of the first open source attempts at an implementation of this architecture. As you'd expect, HBase was designed to run on top of HDFS, giving HDFS environments an option for creating mutable datasets that can utilize indexing.

Partitioning

HBase, unlike other NoSQL solutions, keeps keys and values as raw as possible—keys, columns, cells are all byte arrays. This can be a powerful feature, but it also can lead to complexity.

HBase partitioning defines regions on the byte array of the key, which can make HBase susceptible to skew if keys are badly designed. You can apply hash partitioning, but only if you add hashes to the start of byte array keys.

Mutation options

In the HBase world, a client connects to the HBase master and gets the partition splits. After all of the partition splits are known, the client is free to write to all the partition (region) leaders. HBase, like all NoSQL solutions, allows for single or bulk row mutation. Every cell is a row in the underlying HFiles, so mutation at a cell level is possible.

Optimized read path

HBase is designed for quick reads and writes. Often, only a single seek is required to grab a record from disk if the record is not already cached in memory.

To optimize the read path, HBase has two memory options for caching: there's the *memstore* for caching items as they have just been written, and then there is the *block cache* for caching recently fetched data.

All reads and writes should fall into the low milliseconds, with a given server being able to process anywhere from 30,000 to 100,000 records per second.

Availability versus consistency

HBase is strongly consistent, so if you lose a node, there will be some downtime (generally in the seconds) for a given partition (region). This can make HBase a nonideal selection for real-time applications like websites as compared to Cassandra, which has more flexibility for consistency options.

Primary use case

The primary use case is for a NoSQL store where strong consistency is required. An example of a real-world use case of HBase is an extremely large graph database recording the relationship of stock trades.

In general, HBase is suitable for applications requiring fast mutation, fast fetches, data ordering, and dynamic column creation.

Additionally, HBase is often compared to Cassandra. We talk about Cassandra and its benefits next, but there are a few things about HBase that provide advantages over Cassandra:

- Storage density per node can be much higher; there are production HBase deployments with 30-plus TB on a node, whereas Cassandra is really recommended for only a maximum 5 TB per node. This is mainly because HBase was built to run on HDFS, which was designed from the start to support larger node capacities.
- Batch writing operations with HBase are much easier to scale. The Cassandra default batching mechanics can cause problems as the cluster goes, primarily because Cassandra doesn't have an elected leader for a region like HBase does.
- Recovery from failure is easier. In Cassandra, when you lose a node, you must replace it (which is pretty easy with autoscaling groups), but HBase just repartitions and keeps going.

Apache Cassandra

Although Cassandra is targeted at similar use cases as HBase, it takes a somewhat different approach in its design.

Genealogy

About the same time HBase was released, Facebook was working on its own NoSQL store called Cassandra. Originally, the big difference between the two was the consistency model—whereas HBase uses strong consistency, Cassandra provides a tunable consistency model (see the upcoming sidebar for more on this).

Tunable Consistency

Earlier, we talked about the CAP theorem and how you have a choice between strong or eventual consistency. Although that rule still holds, you can bend the rules a good deal. To explain this, let's look at how Cassandra does this with different write and read configurations.

One Write and One Read

In Cassandra, you can define how many nodes need to be involved in a read or a write confirmation. The fastest option is one node per write and one per read, which would look like Figure 5-10.

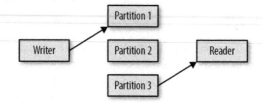

Figure 5-10. Cassandra consistency with single-node writes and reads

Figure 5-10 illustrates that if you read right after you write, there is a chance that you'll get old results because the write might not have been replicated to the partition from which it is being read.

Note that with this model, you could lose two partitions to failure, and read and write behavior would not be affected, which is a benefit of eventual consistency. Additionally, any pattern with only one write has a much higher chance of data loss. If you lose the node that you are writing to before the data is replicated or saved to disk, there is a chance of data loss.

Quorum Read and Write

If the number of writes and reads is greater than the number of partitions, we can get consistency of read after write. With more reads/writes than replications, you are always guaranteed to have at least one of the reads overlap with one of the writes. One example of this would be two writes and two reads, which would look something like Figure 5-11.

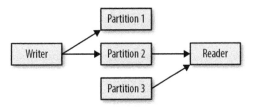

Figure 5-11. Cassandra consistency with multiple reads and writes

From this diagram, we see that the reader will read from partitions 2 and 3. Partition 3 might have the value, but it might have an older timestamp than partition 2, so the reader will take the partition 2 version over the partition 3 version.

Now if we lose a node, we're still fine because our reading and writing will look like Figure 5-12.

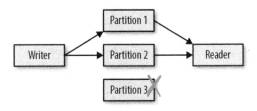

Figure 5-12. Cassandra consistency during node loss

This is that gray area with the CAP theorem because we are experiencing failure but we are not losing availability. The reason this still holds is that Cassandra in this configuration has extended the definition of failure in the way that CAP cares about it. In the Quorum configuration, a failure is the loss of two nodes.

This stretching of the CAP theorem doesn't come without cost. There is a performance hit compared to a strongly consistent system. Figure 5-13 comparing HBase and Cassandra quorum write configuration helps illustrate this.

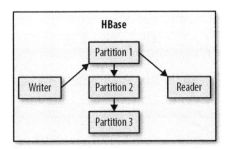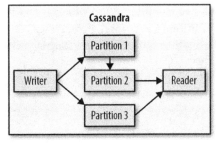

Figure 5-13. HBase versus Cassandra consistency

Note that in the HBase solution there is a leader, and this allows the writer and reader to always have to talk to only one node, whereas the Cassandra quorum configuration requires two.

Other Options

There are other Cassandra configuration options. For example, you could have three write operations and one read, or one write and three reads, as shown in Figure 5-14. This will allow you to focus the performance hit on one side or the other.

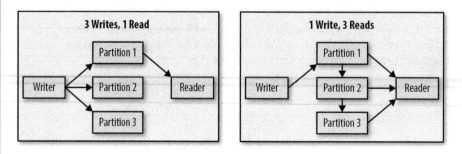

Figure 5-14. Cassandra consistency—other configuration options

Additionally, Cassandra can even change the definition of failure beyond a node. You could build a quorum between clusters, so if you had three clusters, you could lose a single cluster and not be affected. There are, however, additional performance penalties for this type of configuration.

Cassandra also differentiated itself by offering a query language called *CQL*, making it easier for users to work with data in Cassandra by providing a familiar SQL-like interface. Also, Cassandra isn't tied to HDFS as the underlying data store, providing more flexibility for deployments.

Partitioning

Like HBase, Cassandra has range partitioning. Unlike HBase, Cassandra doesn't require manual definition of keys, and instead hashes everything behind the scenes. In addition, Cassandra, through CQL, allows for simple manual partitioning and ordering through a two-key grouping scheme at table creation.

Figure 5-15 shows an example of a table creation in Cassandra using two keys.

```
CREATE TABLE stock_trades (
    stock_id bigint,
    day_year_of_trade int          Multipart partition primary key
    time_of_day_of_trade int,
    Price double,                    ╱
    PRIMARY KEY ((stock_id, day_year_of_trade), time_of_day_of_trade)
)
                                            ╱
                              Field to sort by within a
                              partitioned primary key
```

Figure 5-15. Creating a Cassandra table with two keys

This will partition the records by stock and year/day. Then, within that partition, all of the prices will be ordered by time. The important thing to note is just how easy it is to configure this type of table compared to a system like HBase.

This simple partitioning might be the most important difference between HBase and Cassandra. HBase really requires you to know how to write code to do just about anything with it. With Cassandra, if you understand SQL, you can become productive in little time. However, as with any interface, you will need to quickly learn what is happening behind the scenes of your CQL before you can reach high performance.

Mutation options

For the most part, Cassandra write patterns will feel very much like HBase, focused on fast single-record updates.

Optimized read path

Considering the read path, Cassandra is again very much like HBase but more focused on tunable consistency. In addition, Cassandra can read from any replicas, whereas HBase must write and read to a partitions leader node. Cassandra can read and write to any of a record's replica nodes.

Primary use case

Cassandra will generally be suitable for any use case for which HBase is a fit. The primary considerations for selecting Cassandra versus HBase will focus on consistency models and differences in failure handling.

Elasticsearch and Apache Solr

Continuing our discussion of systems that are targeted at specific use cases, we next look at Lucene-based systems such as Solr and Elasticsearch.

Genealogy

Lucene is an open source project created to index web content in order to facilitate implementation of web search engines. Elasticsearch and Solr are two implementations of query engines built on top of Lucene, providing functionality to serve up Lucene results.

Partitioning

Hash partitioning is key here. Because most query operations in these engines are reduce-by-key queries, the perfect partitioning enabled by the hash gives these systems good storage and queryable partitioning. Because every document has an ID and all hashing is performed on that ID, these systems eliminate problems with data skew.

Mutation options

The ability to update documents in these systems somewhat varies between the systems and specific version. Generally speaking, the ability to update documents is supported, either entire documents or specific fields in documents. However, in the background this might require deleting the old document and replacing with a new version.

Note that this model for mutating data can lead to increased storage requirements because of the need to store different versions of a document while updating. This can also mean increased query times while documents are updating. If your requirements include high mutability of data, a Lucene-based search tool might not be an optimal choice because of these performance considerations.

Optimized read path

Whereas a NoSQL system allows you to query a record by its primary key, and in some cases possibly a secondary key, Lucene-based systems can query their documents by any indexed field. In addition, a Lucene engine is not just about getting a record; it is primarily a search engine, so what ends up being returned and in which order is highly important.

In addition, there is the whole idea of faceting, in which we are not requesting records but counts to generate charts based on the index counts. These facets have become extremely popular with the rise of dynamic charting tools like Kibana (for Elasticsearch), Banana (for Solr), or Hue, which supports multiple systems. These UIs lower the bar to getting value out of data in these systems.

Primary use case

If you need a search engine or real-time cubing on your data, these are suitable tools. However, note that all of the indexing makes these systems expensive for storage and long-term data retention. So, although these systems are extremely useful, they can be difficult to scale.

Newcomers: Apache Kudu and CockroachDB

In the open source enterprise data world, it isn't every day that new ideas come up and become successful. This section discusses two relatively new solutions: Apache Kudu and CockroachDB.

Kudu

Kudu is a Spanner-type system that comes out of Cloudera. Inspired by the initial promise of Parquet and all of the benefits we get from columnar file types, Kudu feels very much like HBase and Parquet had a baby. The idea here is that Kudu will have scan speeds closer to HDFS along with the mutability of a NoSQL solution. However, it is unlikely that it will be faster or better at scans than HDFS or that it will perform mutations and single-record access like a NoSQL.

The underlying storage is a columnar format that helps with scans at the expense of PUTs and GETs given that the columnar format needs to write every column in a different file or location—in Kudu's case, it is in a different file. This means if you have 100 columns, you have 100 seeks on disk to get one record with a GET. If you are planning on doing this on a spindle, it would take forever to do basic PUTs and GETs, so solid-state drives (SSDs) might be recommended when using Kudu.

Because of these limitations, Kudu is mostly a fit for data that needs to be mutated in near real time. For the most part, we won't discuss Kudu specifically, but we do reference tables for scanning, which could be tables on HDFS, S3, or Kudu.

CockroachDB

This one has possibly the oddest named of all the storage platforms. The idea is that cockroaches are hard to kill, and so is this storage platform. You can think of CockroachDB as a cross between Impala and Kudu but with transactions and nested types. Whereas with Kudu the SQL layer is independent from the storage system, CockroachDB is more like Cassandra or a traditional relational database in that it has SQL as a core way to interact with the system.

As we just noted, CockroachDB stands out among the Spanner open source solutions in that it offers transactions with both snapshot isolation and serializable snapshot isolation, which is a valuable mechanism to maintain data integrity. The sidebar that follows provides more details on the different transaction types to help understand the distinction.

Snapshot Isolation Versus Serializable Isolation

Although transactions are an integral part of traditional data management systems like relational databases, they're not as common with open source distributed data management systems. So, to help illustrate the differences in isolation types with transactions, let's use an example from database expert Jim Gray. In this example, you have a bag of four balls: two black and two white. Then, you execute the following two mutations and commit:

- Change all white balls to black.
- Change all black balls to white.

Here is the timeline of when the transactions start and finish:

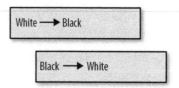

In the serializable example, the two commands would execute one after the other, as shown in Figure 5-16.

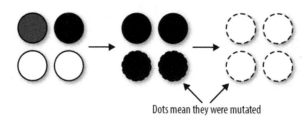

Figure 5-16. Transactions with serializable isolation

In the case of snapshot isolation, you would see a different result as the commands are firing in parallel and they are mutating different balls independently, as shown in Figure 5-17.

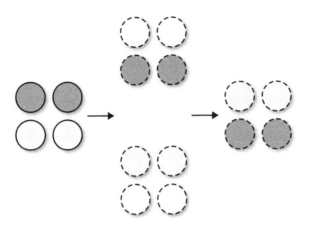

Figure 5-17. Transactions with snapshot isolation

In-Memory Storage Systems

The last type of storage system we look at in this chapter is in-memory stores. We should note that most storage solutions we have talked about will utilize some type of memory layer for caching and/or buffering. Additionally, there are many commonly used systems for data caching as part of the application layer; for example, Memcached or Oracle Coherence. In this case, we're talking about long-term storage systems that make in-memory storage a core part of their storage. This is a large category, and we won't be able to cover them all. Instead, we are going to cover only two that will provide good representations of the features provided by an in-memory storage system, specifically:

- Druid, which provides high-performance parallel operations
- Redis, which supports advanced data structures

We should also note that streaming engines such as Spark Streaming, Flink, or Kafka Streams could also be viewed as providing similar functionality because they provide persistent state within the engine. In this chapter, we're focused on storage systems, but we'll spend some time discussing these streaming engines in Chapter 8.

Druid.io

We begin by describing Druid, which occupies the same state as systems like OpenTSDB, InfluxDB, and Facebook's Beringei. The difference that Druid brings to the table is offering a large distributed cache layer that supports cross-metric aggregation. Let's walk through how this is different from a normal time-series database. In something like OpenTSDB, metrics are stored next to one another on disk, as depicted in Figure 5-18.

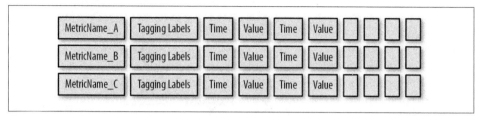

Figure 5-18. OpenTSDB metric storage

If you want to aggregate a bunch of metrics, you will need to seek each one of these metrics and then perform a merge join. In the typical use case of aggregating CPU usage across a distributed system, this could translate to thousands or millions of metrics being added or averaged together. In your typical time-series system, this would not only require a large number of queries that could produce seeks on disk, but the aggregation might not be happening in a distributed way, as is illustrated in Figure 5-19.

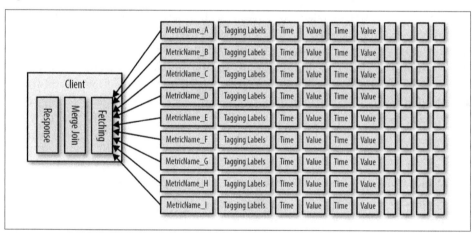

Figure 5-19. Distribution in a time-series database

The Druid architecture, in contrast, looks like Figure 5-20.

The thing to note here is that recent data is in memory, and querying it happens in a distributed manner, removing seeks and solving for the distributed aggregation problem. Also note that Druid utilizes on-disk storage for older data, so it's not solely an in-memory system.

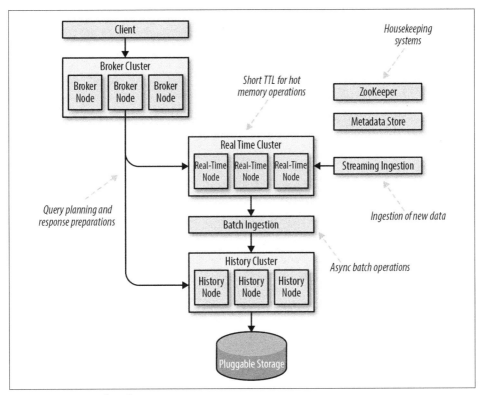

Figure 5-20. Druid architecture

Redis

Redis is a very popular in-memory system that offers a wide range of data structures. Although this type of in-memory data store can suffer from cost and limited data density on a given node, it can provide advantages by supporting advanced data structures.

Redis is well suited for use as a caching layer; for example, to provide a session cache for an online application. Additionally, the list and set functionality provided by Redis can support features such as the following:

- Add an entity ranked by a score
- Get the rank of a given entity
- Page up or down from a given rank
- Update the entity and move it along the ranking

A common example of where you might apply this would be creating a dynamic leaderboard; for example, a list of top scorers for an online game.

To do these operations in HDFS, S3, or a NoSQL offering wouldn't be easy at all. Even though NoSQLs provide ordering with indexing and storage of data, they will not be able to match the speed that an in-memory data store like Redis can provide.

Summary

In this chapter, we provided a framework for evaluating open source enterprise storage systems. This framework uses a set of criteria to categorize storage systems and ultimately provide guidance toward selecting specific systems for your data architectures. These considerations include how the systems partition data, how they support mutations of data, how data is accessed, and consistency versus availability models. These considerations lead us to defining the primary use cases for which these systems are suitable.

It's impossible, of course, to cover every available system and every use case, but using the framework provided in this chapter should facilitate the design of optimal architectures to build your data solutions.

CHAPTER 6

The Meta of Enterprise Data

Meta is an interesting word that tends to be used in different ways, but in the context of this discussion, it's information that provides higher-level context and descriptions about some related information. To talk about a domain outside of data, we can look at the video gaming and e-sports world, where it's common to hear people talk about the "meta" of a game. In the video gaming context, this term is used to refer to a strategy and approach to the game within the game. People who understand the "metas" and can utilize them are far more successful in winning in video games then those who play for fun.

In the world of data, metadata is the information and strategy surrounding data and the use of that data. This metadata will allow additional visibility into things like what data is being stored, what it's being used for, and who's using it. In some cases, metadata can be more important than the data itself, and it's not uncommon for the metadata to outlive the actual data. Effective metadata management is a critically important part of building data solutions, so in this chapter, we talk about planning for and managing the implementation of a metadata solution in your data applications.

It's worth noting that managing metadata is probably one of the most difficult challenges to address when designing a data solution. This can be attributed to the vast number of sources, ingestion options, storage systems, and access patterns involved in complex data systems. Additionally, newer enterprise data management systems facilitate user access to data for process and analysis, which can mean the continual creation of new datasets to catalog.

However, the benefits of a robust metadata solution outweigh the complexity and difficulty of implementing that solution, and there is no better time than now to begin planning it out. It's a lot easier to apply a strategy as you build out your solution than to apply it retroactively. Putting in the effort in the project planning stages will go a long way toward ensuring the creation of successful and manageable data projects.

Peanut Butter in Your Hair

While working at Cloudera, one of the authors overheard a statement about peanut butter and hair, which stuck with him (pun intended). This occurred while working with an interface design team and trying to expedite the process of defining an API for nested types. At this point, somebody made this observation: "Building interfaces is like putting peanut butter in your hair. It's really easy to put peanut butter into your hair, but really hard to get it out."

It may be difficult to see how this relates to the topic of metadata, but it is very easy to imagine the frustration of trying to clean a glob of peanut butter from your hair. The point here is the importance of doing things right when you're building out an infrastructure that needs to last. All of this planning might sound counter to following an Agile process. However, when building out an enterprise data infrastructure that's going to last for years, there are areas where speed makes sense, but there are areas where more forethought is important. Metadata management is definitely one of those areas where it's better to take the time to ensure a robust process.

Reasons to Care About Metadata

Before discussing the hows of metadata management, let's talk some more about the whys. Having a successful metadata strategy will provide value to your business across three crucial dimensions: visibility into your data, relationships between that data, and regulations relating to that data.

Visibility

Over the past 10 or so years, we've worked with a large number of companies, and one of the things that typifies the maturity of a company's data practice is whether the company knows what data it collects and how to access it. One category of metadata is a catalog of all data collected, in which the catalog includes items such as the names of fields, what each field represents, lineage of the field, and so on. Any data worker in the company should have access to this catalog (with appropriate security restrictions applied).

This can enable a number of positive outcomes with data:

Faster time to market for data products
> Just knowing what data exists and where the data is so you don't need to waste time trying to find the data or create new data collection pipelines.

Avoiding duplication of work

When multiple departments or teams need similar data, duplicating the effort to collect the data would be wasteful. Having access to a catalog of available data will help avoid this waste of time and effort.

Deriving more value

One of the larger problems in getting value from data is figuring out just what value can be derived from available data. With more visibility into what data is collected, data scientists and analysts are able to gain more insight into the types of problems that can be explored and solved with that data.

Identifying gaps

Knowing what data you have is directly related to knowing what you don't have but should. The more visibility you have into your data, the easier it becomes to identify these gaps.

Relationships

A by-product of having increased visibility into your data is the ability to see how different datasets can relate. Understanding these relationships can help you to develop complex use cases across different entity types.

An example of entity relationships that might be useful in a system architecture could be the metadata around hardware and software locations. To further illustrate this, we'll use the example of a commercially available Hadoop management solution. In this case, we have a data model with many entities, including the following:

- Cluster nodes
- Racks
- Applications
- Services

With these entities, we're able to use the Hadoop management system to derive an entity relationship diagram using tagged fields that looks like something you see for a relational model. This is illustrated in Figure 6-1.

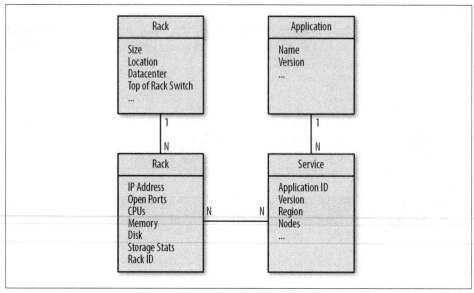

Figure 6-1. Entity relationship diagram for a Hadoop cluster

With knowledge of these relationships, you can now do a couple of things:

Traversal
> You can travel down any of the lines to discovery other entities. Think about starting at a rack and figuring out what applications are running on that rack.

Rollups
> You can aggregate or sum statuses or issues within a block of entities. Think about the rack-to-application example; you might be able to trace multiple application outages to a top-of-rack switch going out because you understand the relationships between those applications and the affected rack.

Now, let's take our example to the next level and add more entities, such as these:

- Kafka topics
- Database tables
- Queries (including input and output)
- Stream processing operations
- Source data generators

The idea is to have enough entities to tell the complete story of your data; how did it come in, where is it stored, how is it used, what is being done with the outputs, and so on.

Regulation

Considerations around regulation are becoming increasingly critical when planning your data projects. Let's look at some of the contributing factors:

Data volume
> The amount of data being collected increases exponentially every year. This of course includes personal data.

Exposure
> As data collection on all of us has grown, we've seen increasing numbers of very visible hacking incidents affecting millions of people. As we collect more data and that data has more value, protecting it has become even more difficult. As the value of data increases, the efforts to illegally obtain and misuse it will also increase.

Power
> The power that data can offer companies and governments is very clear. The question now is how much power should companies and governments be granted when it comes to data collection and usage? A good example is the Russian intrusion into the 2016 US electoral process. As these concerns become more pressing, it's safe to assume that the calls for regulation and oversight of data will grow.

Regulatory responses

We're already beginning to see regulatory response to concerns around the negative impacts of all this data collection. For example, the General Data Protection Regulation (GDPR) created by the European Union mandates that companies have policies in place to deal with issues such as those discussed in the following subsections.

Right to personal information. This allows any person to request from any company details on the data that the company has about them. The impact of this request to data systems is potentially very significant. You need to not only know where all of the data for a person is stored in your company, but also figure out how to query it in an efficient manner and how to present it without giving away any of the confidential information about your internal data systems.

Right to be forgotten. This allows any person to request from any company that the company remove all data related to them or correct the data. This also has the potential to present a significant impact to your systems.

Restriction on applications of data. This restricts companies to using collected data only for certain purposes that have been clearly expressed in the company's terms of service to which a person has consented. This affects data systems in that it requires companies to collect information on the types of processing that is being performed with specific data.

Exposure impact assessment.   It will be necessary for companies to quickly understand which data has been compromised in the event of a hack. Knowing which data has been collected and where it is will be critical to be able to provide this type of assessment. This touches on all of the aforementioned considerations: knowledge of the data, relationships within the data, understanding what access and processing is happening on the data, and so on.

Having metadata will be critical to complying with regulatory requirements such as those already mentioned. For example, you can't comply with the right-to-be-forgotten rules if you don't know what data you've collected on a specific customer and where that data is located.

Types of Metadata in a Data Architecture

We've talked about why metadata is important, and hopefully made the case for why you should have a good metadata strategy in place. Let's now talk about types of metadata we'll need to be concerned with to have a viable strategy. This includes the following categories of data:

Data at rest
> This is metadata about data that's been ingested into storage on disk (or memory in some specialized cases). This can include long-term storage, such as the Hadoop Distributed File System (HDFS), or shorter-term storage such as a Kafka topic.

Data in motion
> Generally speaking, this is data that's moving through a data pipeline.

Metadata for source data (entities)
> This includes things such as the entity types we talked about in the section "Relationships" on page 121.

Metadata about data processing
> Metadata about processing of data. We can also refer to this as *operational metadata*.

Reports and dashboards
> Metadata describing prepared reports that are part of a system.

Data at Rest

Data at rest refers to data that's in long-term storage in a system; for example, things like tables and fields in a database, collections in a Lucene-based system, metrics in a time-series database, or files in filesystems or object stores. Think about metadata at this layer as a catalog of what data is available.

Typically, the way that we store metadata about this type of data is to tag it with meaningful, searchable, and indexable data. Let's look at an example of a customer purchase table in Table 6-1. The database name is Purchasing.

Table 6-1. Example customer receipts table

Field	Type
User_id	Long
Receipt_num	Long
Item_purchased_id	Long
Amount	Decimal(7,2)
Timestamp	Timestamp
Method	String
Card_id	Long
Purchased_port	String

Each field and type presented in Table 6-1 is metadata about the database, table, and fields. At a minimum, we'd want to store this metadata and make it accessible, maybe through a Lucene-based system or a metadata repository like the Hive metastore. But there is more metadata that can be captured; for example:

Audit logs
　　How the table was created and a history of changes to the table.

Comments
　　Comments on the table and fields.

Tagging
- Tagging fields if they contain personal data such as User_id and Card_id.
- Tagging joinable tables. Suppose that the Card_id is a unique identifier because we want to hide the actual card number from queries. To ensure that users of the database understand how to perform a join to extract the card number, we should apply a tag to the Card_id field to reference which table should be joined against to get the real identifier.
- Details such as data owners.

Access rights
　　Who is allowed access to this table.

Usage

What queries and users are accessing this table.

Sources

Lineage for the data; for example, is it gathered from a source system, or is the data in this table the result of transformational jobs?

Data in Motion

Now that we've considered metadata for data at rest, let's look at metadata for data on its way to storage. There are a number of ways that we can ingest data in modern data architectures, so let's examine some of those.

Batch delivery

In batch delivery, we send data at intervals, and it is put into our systems in large batches of records. Some common ways of sourcing data in batch is through FTP, SCP, or a handoff to an object store. This data might be delivered as a CSV, JSON, binary, and so on, and will normally be compressed. This might look something like Figure 6-2.

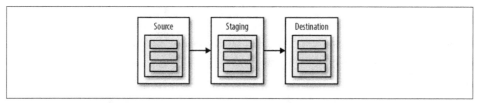

Figure 6-2. Batch data delivery

Streaming or microbatching

With streaming, or microbatching, data is continuously moving through the system; for example, sensor data in an Internet of Things (IoT) use case. Typically, somewhere in the pipeline there will be some form of scalable pipe such as a message queue or Kafka, followed by a service to provide transformations over streaming data and ingestion to the target location. This might look like Figure 6-3.

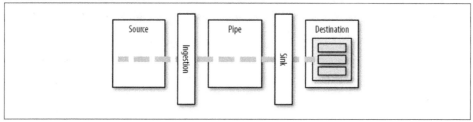

Figure 6-3. Streaming data delivery

Application operations

In this architecture, data stores are directly connected to an application, and the application is directly writing to those data stores. However, it is becoming more common that operational data stores are separated from analytical data stores. This means that even if an application has an operational data store, it will also use batching or streaming to push data to an external analytical data store. This type of workflow is illustrated in Figure 6-4.

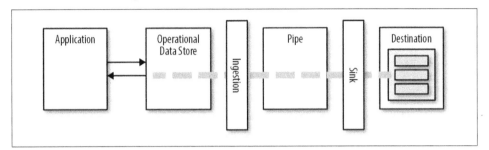

Figure 6-4. Data delivery between applications and data stores

Post transformation

This is when data is created from an already existing dataset (Figure 6-5). Normally, we do this with SQL or a distributed processing engine like Apache Spark. These processing jobs could be production jobs or something a user fired off as part of an ad hoc session.

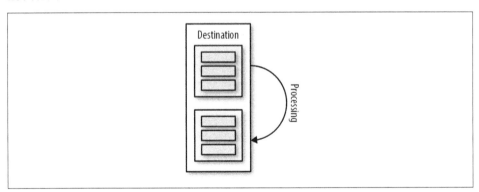

Figure 6-5. Dataset creation from an existing dataset

Metadata to capture for data in motion

As you can see, there are lots of entry points to data pipelines. We need to understand all of these entry points and catalog them to successfully capture the metadata. It's important to understand the lineage of data stored in the system. Let's go into some of the things that we will want to capture as we collect metadata about the movement and possible transformation of data.

Paths. We will want to label the path that data takes through the system. Figure 6-6 shows that the path through a system can include numerous components such as source systems, data collection systems, data routing, transformations, and so forth. We discuss specific metadata considerations for some components in the following sections.

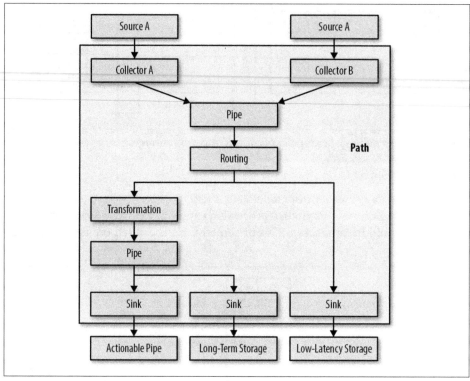

Figure 6-6. Example path through a data pipeline

Sources. As we just discussed, the sources are where the data is coming from. These will often be external systems, but they can also be internal systems or an existing data source or feed.

Data movement. This defines the routes data will take. Normally, this describes whether the data is forked, or sent to more than one place. For example, Figure 6-6 illustrates where the initial pipe is sent both to a transformation and directly to a sink and target storage.

We talk a lot about routing in Chapter 7, but for now, think about routing as the path the data takes from sources to destinations. Figure 6-7 shows a basic example where we're receiving data from multiple sources via Kafka. The input data is then routed to multiple target storage systems based on certain criteria such as the type of the data or intended use for the processed data.

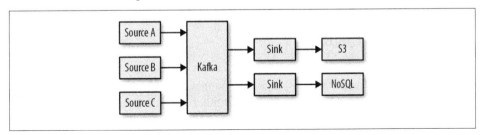

Figure 6-7. Routing multiple data sources

In Figure 6-7, routing metadata would tell us that data from source B is going through Kafka and landing in S3 and a NoSQL system. This is a simplistic example; in the real world, routing would probably include filtering of data, modifications to the data, and so on.

Transformations. This is documentation around how the data is being transformed. Here are some of the factors we want to document:

Format changes
> What is the underlying data structure for the source data and then after any transformations? For example, the source data might be JSON, but the target format is protocol buffers.

Data fidelity
> Is data filtered out or changed in a way that makes it no longer full fidelity?

Atomic, joined, sessioned, or context
> Is the transformation based on only the input record, or is there additional context from external data?

Job metadata
> Basic information about the processing jobs: name, technologies used, production status, version number, project owner, SLAs, and so on.

Lineage of field metadata
> Earlier in the chapter we talked about field metadata/tagging. As we input fields into our transformation to produce new fields, we need to be able to track the lineage of that tagging and metadata. A good example is a field that contains personally identifiable information (PII). If fields are generated by a transformation

and the sources contain PII fields, the existence of the historical PII data should be captured in the new field.

Destinations. This documents the landing zone for the data. This should line up with the metadata we have already talked about in the earlier section about data at rest. In fact, this meta information should be added or linked to the destination metadata.

Metadata for Source Data

Just as our destinations need metadata, we'll also want to consider metadata for our data sources. Now, if you have only one source, this might seem like overkill, but the chances are that you'll collect data from a number of sources: cell phones, servers, sensors, databases, and so forth. We'll want to capture metadata about these sources just as carefully as the metadata in our systems.

Just to further convince you, here are some reasons to capture this metadata:

Understand what is submitting data to our system
> Think about the cell phone world; you will want to know the types of phones (model, memory, CPU, etc.) or where they are located (signal strength, distance from cell towers). This information might help you understand how to improve service.

Identification of malicious activity
> When you have sources that number in the millions—for example, an IoT use case—there's a chance that someone may want to attack your system. Understanding your sources could offer solutions to identify these bad actors and address them separately from real sources.

Relationships
> Suppose that you're monitoring hardware and looking for the impact of failure. In this case, you'll want metadata about the relationship and location of servers to racks and switches. This would also apply to IoT use cases for which you are getting inputs from many sensors in a larger system like a car or a plane.

Metadata About Data Processing

The data processing that might occur in your systems could be anything from simple SQL queries to advanced Apache Spark Jobs, machine learning, and so on. Additionally, because of the variety of processing technologies, it will be difficult to capture which ones are being used and for what purposes. You'll want to at least make sure you're getting the basics, which will provide a basis from which to build:

Access
> What is accessing specific data?

Frequency

How often is the data being accessed?

Output

Is the data getting sent outside the system or to another table in the system?

Technology used

Some technologies like SQL will leave a clear audit trail, whereas other things might be more difficult to track; for example, Apache Spark jobs. A Spark job's logic is hidden in Java/Scala/Python code, which is difficult to interpret with auditing tools.

Note that capturing this metadata is more critical for production jobs that are producing real, actionable output. For jobs that are used for testing, research, and so on. it's reasonable to use judgment as to how much needs to be captured. On the other hand, regulations such as GDPR don't differentiate between production and development environments, so this is something to keep in mind for planning.

For production jobs, consider making the source code accessible; for example, in a version control system such as a company GitHub repository. This will allow you to review the code.

It's worthwhile to give special consideration to machine learning jobs, given that as algorithms become more complex, it can become more difficult to understand how these algorithms are making decisions. As models become harder to understand, the chances of undesirable and even unethical results can increase, putting your company at risk. Consider capturing the following:

Purpose of the model

What's the use case at which the model is targeted?

Technology and algorithm used

An example would be Spark MLlib or TensorFlow used to perform a k-means clustering job.

Input features

Think of features as input to machine learning algorithms. For example, specific data attributes selected from an input dataset to use as input features for k-means clustering.

Training/test dataset

This is the data that is used to train, validate, and test your models.

Training goals for optimal state

This is defining the goals that are used to evaluate the success of the model. These goals will be highly dependent on application requirements, algorithms, and so on; for example, the classification accuracy for a classification model.

Human adjustments to the model
Some models can be modified by human input. For any models for which this occurs, it's important to capture what and why these adjustments were made.

Model owners
Who are the individuals responsible for implementation, definition, and so forth for the deployed model?

Reports and Dashboards

Some common outputs of processing are human-readable reports and dashboards. These are very easy to create, but they also quickly become outdated.

As part of your metadata strategy, you should be capturing at least the following for visible, actionable reports:

- Data sources
- Any data transformations
- Information on the report's creator
- Log of modifications
- Purpose of report
- Tags about what it relates to

Tags can help map reports back to what they're reporting about. Examples might include tags relating to regions, location, versions, and so on. Because an organization might have hundreds to thousands of dashboards, tagging can be a tool for linking dashboards back to the things they are reporting on, potentially reducing duplicate report generation.

Metadata Collection

We noted at the beginning of this chapter that metadata collection is challenging, and the fact is many companies don't have effective processes in place to capture all of the metadata they should be collecting. Companies will normally fall into the following categories in terms of metadata management:

Multiple silos
This is when a company has many groups, each of which is at a different level of maturity in terms of metadata management, often with little to no cross-group visibility into available metadata.

Centralized knowledge
In this case, a limited number of people have access to or knowledge of datasets.

The periodic census

These are companies that have a data directory that is manually maintained and is almost always out-of-date. Maybe once a year or every couple of years, they will send people around to catalog and document the datasets that exist within the organization and produce a database or even a spreadsheet that will rapidly become out-of-date.

The deliberate

These companies have a strategy from day one about data collection and data generation. All metadata is up-to-date all the time as much as possible because of company policies and processes. We will use these companies as a model in this section.

Let's now dig into two approaches commonly used together to set up a deliberate metadata collection strategy: declarative and discovery. *Declarative* is the collection of data through the normal actions of using the system, whereas *discovery* is the effort to figure out what happened after the fact.

Declarative Metadata Collection

The idea of declarative metadata management is that you require and enable metadata to be created as new data sources are added to the system or as the use or movement of the data is altered. This way, we can gather the metadata from the persons or groups that are involved in collecting it.

Declarative collection can happen only if the tools used to onboard the data or manage the route or use of the data are active in reporting the changes to the metadata solution. This is most likely implemented by limiting these operations to paths that are approved and fully integrated into the metadata solution. The methods to achieve this will be dependent on specific tools.

We note that declarative collection requires limiting data operations to approved paths. This can sound burdensome given that no one loves being forced to rigidly follow processes. We can avoid making this a burden by enabling processes to facilitate this collection. It's useful at this point to recall some of the more challenging characteristics of data pipelines:

They're not simple

To do data ingestion, processing, and so on correctly, you need things such as monitoring, transformation, scaling, and failover.

They'll likely utilize relatively standardized architectures

We talked about batch and streaming use cases, and although there are different ways to implement either, in most cases you can support the majority of use cases with a limited number of implementations.

Making data pipelines easier to use can facilitate building declarative metadata collection into the pipeline. Some ways we could make pipelines easier to use include the following:

Requiring ingestion be declared through a vendor tool
> For example, you could use the Confluent Schema Registry to capture all the schema-related information and to feed your metadata solution with information (as part of allowing the schema registration).

Requiring use of the Hive Metastore
> Using the Hive Metastore or another central metastore for tables could be key to a declarative approach if it is integrated with your metadata solution and reports mutations as part of the mutation process.

The main idea for a declarative solution is that the metadata system is triggered on any action done, where an action might be ingesting a dataset, creating a new table from a dataset, or running a transformation on a dataset. When triggered, the tool might send a notification to the metadata system as part of its operations, or the metadata system might read from the managing systems edit logs. Again, however, the way this is accomplished will be dependent on specific solutions.

What metadata should you declare?

When designing a declarative path, you'll want to build in collections of the types of metadata we discussed earlier in this chapter:

- Data sources
- Technologies used
- Table and field names and tags
- Destinations
- Uses of the data
- Owners and/or stewards of the data

The idea is that we want the people closest to the data to be the ones entering this data. These will be the people who know the most about the data, and they likely have a stake in complete and accurate metadata collection. This is also a chance to get more knowledge and context for other linked datasets or potentially avoid duplication of data.

Discovery of Metadata

There will always be cases in which data is created without being declared. This could be due to insufficient collection processes or tools that don't provide a comprehensive solution. So, unlike the declarative solution, the discovery solution is looking at the final data and using scripting patterns to try to figure out what happened.

One area that is very difficult to cover via declarative processes is tables or datasets that are created from other tables or data sources via SQL or other Extract, Transform, and Load (ETL) tools. In these cases, discovery is a good approach. We can do this via information from logs or the jobs to try to figure out inputs and outputs. We can also scan the existing tables to see how they overlap with known tables.

If we find gaps in definition, we have a few options:

Review the metadata on the gap table
> There might be tags or comments on the table that tell us more about the reason for the table and its source. More likely, there will be ownership information and its relationship with a database. This ownership information might give us insight into who to contact or notify about the missing information.

Field content classification
> Numerous tools today use regular expressions and machine learning to sample data within your tables and inform you what is inside your tables. Simple cases are flagging social security numbers, credit card numbers, and telephone numbers. These tools can help not only by adding column/table metadata, but also by giving hints to the lineage of the table. Note that most of these tools will likely be vendor or third-party tools.

Audit trail discovery
> Similar to classification of data fields, tools are available that can use artifacts such as logs, generated tables, and so forth to infer metadata. This allows for the creation of audit logs for data, lineage discovery, and documentation of things like tables and datasets without explicit declaration.

How to handle the undocumented

We talked about a few ways to discover the origins of an undocumented dataset. However, in some cases you might not be able to fully discover the origins, or you might discover an unacceptable outcome. In these cases, we have some options for handling these datasets:

Contact data owner with request
> If you have enough information to find the potential owners, a possible approach might be to reach out to them through emails, messaging, or alerts, with the goal to collect more information or to make alterations.

Lock down the table
> In some cases, the dataset might not be acceptable in its undocumented or documented state. In this condition, a possible option is to lock the table down so that

no one but the admin team can access it. This will result in even the owner of the dataset not being able to access it.

Delete the data

After lockdown, a good pattern is to start a time to live (TTL) timer. If this TTL is reached, simply delete the data.

Audit trail

You need to record and review all notifications, locks, and deletes. Users who break the rules beyond normal means should have corrective actions taken.

Metadata Management in Practice

We've talked in great detail about why metadata is important and what you should be planning for when defining a metadata strategy for your projects. The bigger challenge is determining how to implement a comprehensive metadata strategy. A large part of this challenge comes from the profusion of systems, data sources, data formats, and so on that are likely to be part of a distributed data management system. Unfortunately, finding a single tool to manage metadata across an entire data architecture remains a challenge.

One approach that organizations take to address this challenge is to create their own solution. This, of course, creates another set of challenges in implementing and maintaining a custom solution. A better approach is to explore vendor and third-party solutions. Most of the enterprise data management vendors offer solutions that provide functionality to define metadata, track data lineage, audit operations on data, and so forth. These vendor solutions can provide adequate solutions within the vendor offerings and can be valuable tools to address metadata management within those offerings. Finding solutions that work across offerings can be a bigger challenge, but some data integration vendors are offering products that promise to provide a "single pane of glass" solution to manage metadata across systems. Crafting an effective metadata management approach will require exploring the solutions available based on the vendors or projects that your architectures are based on as well as third-party solutions.

Summary

We've talked in this chapter about the importance of planning for and implementing metadata collections as a core part of your data architectures. There are a number of reasons why this is critical, including regulatory reasons and the maintainability of your system. A successful metadata strategy can help ensure the success of your system. A successful metadata strategy should incorporate the following:

- Identification of datasets requiring metadata management. This should include data at rest (either in long-term or short-term storage), data in motion in a processing pipeline, source data, and data processing and analysis.
- Definition of all metadata to be captured for the different datasets.
- Methods to capture the required metadata, including whether declarative metadata collection or collection via discovery is appropriate.
- Identification of tools to manage the metadata collection—either vendor or third-party solutions.

Failing to implement a solid metadata strategy can result in the following:

- Inability for users to find the data they need.
- Nonstandard mechanisms to get data into and out of the system.
- Valuable data sitting unused because no one knows it's even there.
- Potential legal or regulatory action that could harm your company.

We also talked about special considerations around certain types of metadata, including machine learning models and sensitive data such as personally identifiable or financial data. We wrapped up by talking about different ways to achieve these goals, including the use of tools that support declarative metadata collection or collection via discovery. We also touched on how to identify tools to assist in metadata collection, including vendor and third-party tools.

The main takeaway here is that your metadata should be treated just like any other dataset in your company. It should be correlated, joined, and analyzed for value because in the end that metadata represents how your company works and what it does with data. With data being one of the most important assets of companies today, capturing information about its collection, storage, and use should be equally important.

CHAPTER 7

Ensuring Data Integrity

When working with open source enterprise data management systems, it's common to use multiple storage and processing layers in our data architecture, which often means storing data in multiple formats in order to optimize access. This can even mean duplicating data, which in the past might have been viewed as an antipattern because of expense and complexity, but with newer systems and cheap storage, this becomes much more practical.

What doesn't change is the need to ensure the integrity of the data as it moves through the system from the data sources to the final storage of the data. When we talk about *data integrity*, we mean being able to ensure that the data is accurate and consistent throughout our data pipelines. To ensure data integrity, it's critical that we have a known lineage for all data as it moves through the system.

In this chapter, we discuss what it means to ensure data integrity and provide some examples of how to do this as data moves through our system. In this discussion, we consider what we call *full fidelity* data, which is data that maintains the full context of the source data. This data might be stored in different formats from the source data, but as long as the data can be returned to the original state, we consider it full fidelity. We also consider datasets derived from our original source data; for example, data that's been filtered and aggregated. Regardless of whether the final datasets are full fidelity or derived, maintaining the integrity of that data is critical.

What determines whether our data has full fidelity or is derived is the type of processing that occurs as the data moves through the system. To make this clearer, let's provide some examples of full fidelity and derived datasets:

Full fidelity datasets
- Data compressed with a lossless compression format—this is full fidelity data because the data is still full fidelity but in a compressed form.

- Data converted from one format to another; for example, JSON to protobuf—this again is full fidelity because we're maintaining the full fidelity of the data, only in a different format.

Derived datasets
- Data with columns filtered out—we consider this derived (subset) data because we've maintained the original data but with specific values filtered out.
- Data with rows filtered out—again, we consider this derived data.
- Aggregated data—this also is derived data.

Not everything will necessarily fall neatly into these categories. For example, we might have a dataset that combines the original dataset with appended aggregated columns; in this case, we have full fidelity data in the original columns, while new columns are derived data.

Our intention in this chapter is not to try to cover every data processing scenario, but rather provide some examples to get you thinking about how to design your own data pipelines to ensure the integrity of the data in your systems. We begin by providing some examples of the types of data pipelines you might use in your own systems and describe how they might be designed with an eye toward data integrity.

Examples of Building Data Pipelines to Ensure Data Integrity

Before talking about specific examples, it's useful to categorize the design of data pipelines in two ways: predefined paths and paths derived via discovery.

Predefined paths, as you'd probably expect, are data pipelines that are the result of an analysis and design phase that occurs before implementation of the pipelines. In general, predefined paths are easier to monitor and audit because the processing and modeling of the data is defined before implementation of the pipeline begins. This allows for planning for the required monitoring and controls for the data as it moves through the pipeline.

On the opposite end of the spectrum is the discovery option. You can think of this as a more ad hoc or self-service approach to processing data. In this scenario, we let anyone build any paths on the raw data or selected derived datasets and then utilize software to track the lineage so that auditing can determine the validity of the data after the fact. The problem with this approach is that it can quickly become messy. If your business is heavily audited, we recommend using caution with this method.

To provide a real-world example of what this ad hoc discovery process might involve, consider the widespread use of Apache Hive to create data warehouses over data stored in a system like Hadoop. With Hive, data engineers or administrators might create databases from source data and then provide those databases to users for analysis. Those users can then create their own datasets or derived tables from the provided databases. This provides the benefit of allowing users flexibility in how they use data, but it can lead to a proliferation of tables and datasets of unknown origin and value.

Figure 7-1 provides a visual depiction of the predefined and discovery options and shows where they fit on the productivity versus manageability spectrums.

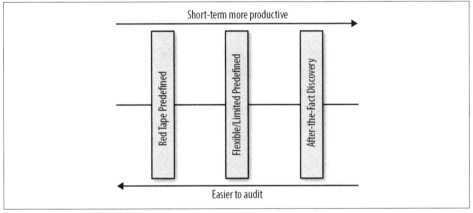

Figure 7-1. Predefined paths versus ad hoc paths

In the end, we most likely will want something in the middle. We'll want some predefined paths that are flexible to change while also creating sandboxes for areas in which freedom of data movement and transition can happen. The trick to making this happen is using validation and interface points. We discussed interfaces extensively in Chapter 4, and we talk more about validation later in this chapter. For now, let's drill down into the predefined and discovery paths.

Predefined Data Pipelines

A predefined pipeline will need to have access points that provide ways to move data into our system and then push that data to the right targets and deliver it in the right formats. As a real-world example of a predefined pipeline, consider the circuit breakers and electrical wiring in your home, as shown in Figure 7-2.

Note that the circuit breaker doesn't care about the source of the power coming into your home, only that the power complies with a specific standard. Then, the circuit breaker and the wiring in your house deliver that power to outlets where you can plug in your various devices. All those devices need to care about is that they can plug in to your house's outlets, and consume power based on expected standards.

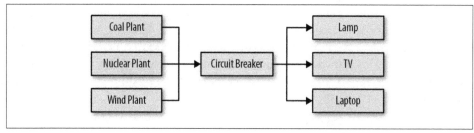

Figure 7-2. Your home's electrical wiring

Similarly, your predefined pipelines need to have the following attributes:

- Well-defined interfaces for input and output in order to support flexibility
- Failover mechanisms for when things go wrong
- Level of guarantee for delivery

Let's consider some real implementations of predefined pipelines that are designed to ensure data integrity: one that handles batch data and one that handles streaming data.

Batch pipeline

A typical predefined batch pipeline might look something like Figure 7-3. Note that this example is assuming an Apache Hadoop–based environment.

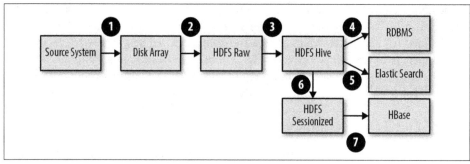

Figure 7-3. Batch pipeline

Let's step through what's happening in this diagram:

1. Data from our source systems is moved into the data pipeline. In this step, the data is just being delivered to a temporary storage array. In some cases, the data could go straight to the long-term storage system (Hadoop Distributed File System, or HDFS, in this example), but the important thing to note is that this is still raw, unchanged data stored in a single system.

2. If the data isn't already in long-term storage (again, HDFS in this example), this is the step at which we move it into long-term storage. At this point, the file is still 100% the same as it was at the source; the only change in this example is that now the data is replicated across HDFS nodes as blocks.

3. This stage uses a processing framework like MapReduce or Spark to add structure to the data and store the data in an Apache Hive optimized–format like Parquet or ORC. It might be possible that this is only a format change, but depending on the input data, there might also be filtering. If there is no filtering, this is still full fidelity data. However, if there is filtering, the resulting data becomes a derived subset of the source data.

4. Data is moved into a relational data store. Note that we've already used the previous step to provide structure to the data, so there should be no data changes other than format changes and possibly filtering.

5. We bulk load data from HDFS into Elasticsearch. Again, there should be no data changes here, only format changes and possibly filtering.

6. Run a Sessionization job on the structured data. The resulting data from this step is no longer full fidelity; instead, it is a derived dataset of the source data.

7. Bulk load the sessionized data from HDFS into HBase. There should be no data changes here, only format changes and possibly filtering. However, because the data it is reading from is no longer full fidelity, the data in HBase will be derived data.

Let's update the diagram in Figure 7-3 to show the state of the data as it moves through the pipeline. This will look like Figure 7-4.

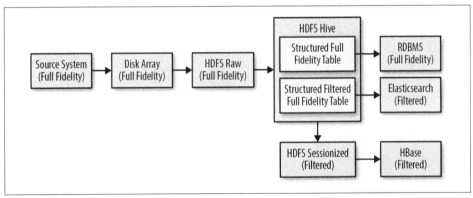

Figure 7-4. Batch pipeline details

Streaming pipeline

An example of a predefined streaming pipeline might look like Figure 7-5. Note the addition of Apache Kafka in this example.

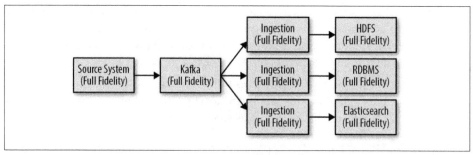

Figure 7-5. Streaming pipeline

We have three separate storage systems here, each of which gets the same data in the same order (with respect to the Kafka partition). This means that the data stays full fidelity throughout the complete ingestion path.

Alternatively, as with the batch architecture, we may want to do enrichment and filtering on the data before it lands in storage. In that case, there are a couple of options. The first option is to add the enrichment and filtering to the ingestion layer, which would look like Figure 7-6.

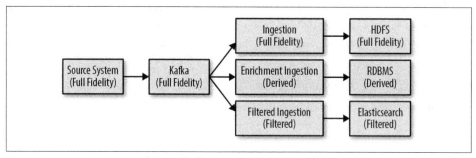

Figure 7-6. Streaming pipeline with filtering and enrichment

Alternatively, there are advantages to adding an additional Kafka layer as shown in Figure 7-7. These advantages include the following:

Partitioning
> We might want to repartition the data in specific ways in order to optimize storage and processing.

Routing
> You need advanced routing logic, which would be inefficient to include in the ingestion layer.

Mutation

> You have requirements for extensive data enrichment that need to be made to multiple datasets, in which case it makes sense to do it once before the ingestion step.

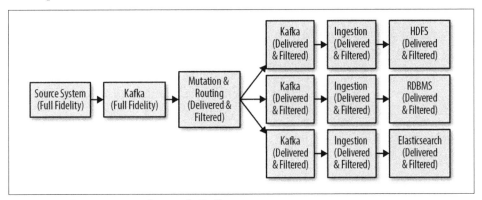

Figure 7-7. Streaming pipeline with Kafka

One thing to avoid is having a single ingestion service for more than one destination, as illustrated in Figure 7-8.

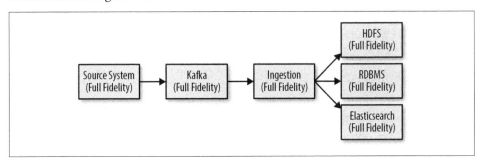

Figure 7-8. Streaming pipeline with multiple destinations

This is bad for a number of reasons:

Monolithic

> These storage systems likely require their own dependencies and libraries. So, writing to all of them from one process will increase the chances for library conflicts.

Complexity

> The simpler and more focused the implementation, the easier it is to test and maintain. Remember, simple is better.

Performance dependencies

> Your ingestion performance will be bound by your slowest storage system.

Rick of systemic failure
> Failure of any one of your storage systems would mean that all data will stop flowing into any of them.

Differing batch sizes
> Different storage systems will be optimized to write in different ways. HDFS and Amazon Simple Storage Service (Amazon S3) will want larger batches, whereas other types of systems will work better with smaller batch sizes.

Difficulty rolling back
> If we ever have a problem in a storage system that requires recovery from a checkpoint, this will be complicated if we're writing to all systems.

Version upgrades
> Upgrades to one storage system could require restarting all of your ingestion nodes.

Validation of Data Pipelines

If you were reading carefully, you noted that all the paths described in the previous section involved some kind of transformation:

At ingestion
> We convert from the raw format to the format used in the destination system.

At enrichment
> We transform or add data in some way.

However, the transformations that occur at these steps can introduce errors that corrupt the integrity of data. So how do we test to confirm that we can trust our system? Let's look at four options: row counts, distinct counts, full-byte comparison, and checksum comparison.

Row Counts

Counting rows might be the easiest method of confirmation as well as the fastest. All it entails is a simple counting of the rows as you write the output data to confirm that the resulting number of records matches the expected count. The problem is it confirms fidelity only in one dimension; it validates that the number of output rows matches the expected value, but it does nothing to confirm what is in the actual records. It is very possible that your row counts match, but one of your columns is null because of a conversion failure, or a number is rounded up and granularity is lost. So, consider this method to be a good first check, but don't rely on it for full validation of data integrity.

Distinct Count

The idea of the distinct count approach is to count the distinct cell values in every column. Think of it as word count for every column in a table, so if you have a table like the one that follows, your distinct count for the second column would be Dog:3 and Cat:4.

1	Dog	Foo
2	Dog	Foo
3	Cat	Foo
4	Dog	Foo
5	Cat	Foo
6	Cat	Foo
7	Cat	Foo

There are three major problems with this approach. First, it cannot validate the order of the unique values. So, if you ran a distinct count on the preceding table and the table that follows, they would match even though they don't retain fidelity, because the Dog and Cat for row 3 and 4 are switched.

1	Dog	Foo
2	Dog	Foo
3	**Dog**	**Foo**
4	**Cat**	**Foo**
5	Cat	Foo
6	Cat	Foo
7	Cat	Foo

The second reason the distinct count approach is not ideal is that it's vulnerable to high-cardinality columns. A *high-cardinality column* is a column with a large number of unique values in it. In our preceding examples, the first column is a nonrepeating ID. This would be very expensive to calculate for a large dataset.

The third reason is that it's overall expensive to do a distinct count compared to a checksum check, which we describe momentarily. Additionally, the checksum approach gives much a much higher confidence of fidelity.

Even through distinct checking is not ideal for checking for full fidelity, it is great for doing an initial sanity check.

Full-Byte Comparison

The most expensive option is to do a full-byte comparison of data. The path in Figure 7-9 describes this.

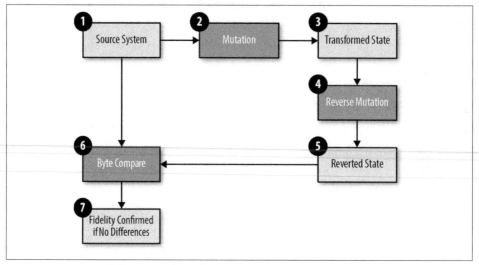

Figure 7-9. Data validation via byte-by-byte comparison

1. Data is consumed from the source and saved in raw form while at the same time passing it to the service that will perform any required transformations or reformatting of the data.

2. Data is transformed and written to the target system.

3. Now the data, in its transformed state, is in the target system, just as in the normal ingestion path.

4. Data is pulled from the target system and transformed back to the raw state again.

5. The original raw data and the reverted raw data are saved to the same storage system.

6. A byte-by-byte comparison is performed with a processing tool such as Apache Spark.

7. If there are no differences, we have validation that the data pipeline maintains data integrity.

Repeat this until you trust your logic. To ensure ongoing validation of data, this process can just be automated and run all the time as part of your processing flow. This will cost more in resources, but it is doable to run this at scale alongside your regular data ingestion processing, assuming that you're willing to devote the expense and resources this requires.

Checksum Comparison

Doing a full-byte comparison might be too expensive to run all the time in your company, but you might still want assurances of data integrity. A relatively easy way to do this is by using checksums on values in the data. So how do we do this?

To provide a very simple example, let's think about two tables, one in a relational database, and one in Hive on Amazon S3. The table in each system looks like the following:

```
CREATE TABLE FOO (
  STR_COL STRING,
  INT_COL INT,
  DOUBLE_COL DOUBLE)
```

You could then run a SQL statement like the following on both tables to confirm that the values are equal:

```
SELECT SUM(HASH(STR_COL)), SUM(INT_COL), SUM(DOUBLE_COL) FROM FOO
```

Now you might argue there is a chance this query could produce matching values when the real values are different. This is possible, as in the following example records:

STR_COL	INT_COL	DOUBLE_COL
A	2	1
B	3	2
C	1	3

If this is a concern for you, let's rewrite our SQL to the following:

```
SELECT SUM(HASH(CONCAT(STR_COL, CONCAT(INT_COL, DOUBLE_COL)))) FROM FOO
```

This way, the checksum is run on the concatenated value of the whole row, providing better assurance that our data is valid. In some edge cases, there might be a mismatch even when the SQL returns matching values. This could happen with differences in hashing functions—if this is a concern, the recommendation for custom hash function implementations applies.

Another concern is the small chance when the hash function of the two databases do not return the same value for the same values. This is not a major cause for concern, but it is most likely caused by different hash implementations on each system. If this does turn out to be the case, the solution is likely implementing user-defined functions to perform the same hashing logic on both systems.

Summary

Data integrity is a critical factor in the design and implementation of any data system. In this chapter, we discussed what we mean by *data integrity* and provided examples of how to implement systems to maintain data integrity and ensure the ability to trace the lineage of data through those systems.

We described what we mean by *full fidelity* versus *derived* when we talk about data, and then described two ways to build data pipelines to ensure integrity based on your requirements:

- *Predefined pipelines*, in which you predefine the path, processing, and so on that data will follow as it moves through your data pipeline.
- *After-the-fact discovery of your data pipeline*, in which you need to define and validate data lineage after it's passed through the system.

We then wrapped up with a discussion of methods to ensure the fidelity of your data, regardless of how that data moves through your system.

CHAPTER 8

Data Processing

Now that we've talked through considerations around building data pipelines, we'll wrap up with a discussion of processing and analyzing all of the data that's been gathered via those data pipelines. Considerations around collecting, storing, and managing data provide the foundation for any data architecture, but it's the processing of that data that that will allow you to derive value.

Just as with other components utilized in a distributed data architecture, the challenge with processing is the large number of options available, many of which have different goals and are targeted at different use cases. Like Chapter 5, the goal of this chapter is to provide a list of criteria for categorizing processing systems in order to provide a framework for evaluating them.

Ultimately, the decisions around selection of specific engines will depend on considerations such as your use cases, experience, and knowledge of your team, target users, SLAs, and components used elsewhere in your architecture. Our hope in this chapter is to provide an understanding of where different tools fit in order to allow you to make more informed decisions when planning your projects.

Attributes of Processing Engines

The following are attributes that we'll use throughout this chapter to distinguish various processing engines:

Directed acyclic graph (DAG) management
How does the engine process an execution plan? We'll provide more detail on what this means momentarily.

Concurrency and compute isolation
How does the system distribute resources to handle multiple users and jobs?

Performance

How fast is the job at executing different types of use cases? Although performance is an important consideration, there can also be trade-offs, such as our next item, fault tolerance.

Fault tolerance

How does the engine respond to failures? Different processing engines will behave differently on job failure. These differences will be important in deciding the suitability of an engine based on your use case.

Interaction model

How do users interact with the system? Do they need to write code in a programming language like Java, or can they interact via a declarative model like SQL?

Batch or streaming

Is the engine designed for processing a large number of records, or for processing single events or small groups of events?

In the following sections, we dig deeper into each of these considerations and discuss where different engines fit. We begin with a discussion of DAG management.

DAG Management

Although the term *directed acyclic graph* sounds intimidating, this is actually a pretty simple concept. A DAG is just a fancy way to refer to a graph in which all the edges between nodes don't offer a path to loop back. In other words, the graph of nodes progresses in a sequence in which every node is directed to a later node in the sequence. In this context, when we talk about graphs, we're not talking about diagrams that visualize numerical quantities, but graphs in the mathematical sense that are composed of vertices and edges.

You can think of a DAG as similar to a query plan; for example, the query plan created by a relational database when it compiles your SQL query. DAGs and query plans are ways to express the work that a distributed engine is going to do to reach the desired goal.

In general, DAG management provided by distributed systems can be broken into the following attributes:

- Whether DAG management is external or built-in to the engine
- Whether management of the DAG is driven by a single driver or multiple drivers

Let's look at these considerations in more detail.

External DAG management

This is the simplest implementation because the engine doesn't know anything about the DAG. Most modern processing engines no longer use this model, and the main engine where you'll still see this model used is MapReduce. Although MapReduce is still a core part of projects like Apache Hadoop, its use has been increasingly eclipsed by more modern and efficient engines like Apache Spark. However, because Map-Reduce was once the primary means to implement distributed processing applications, it's well worth providing an overview both for a historical perspective, and to understand the lineage of systems that have followed.

If you've been working in the distributed data space for a few years, you can likely skip the sidebar that follows. Otherwise, let's go through a quick overview of Map-Reduce.

MapReduce

In general, MapReduce, as you might expect, is made up of different processing stages referred to as *mappers* and *reducers*. Mappers read in data from a data source, apply transformations to the data, and/or sort and then partition the data through a process called a *shuffle*. Shuffles are a fundamental part of distributed data processing, providing the basis for operations such as joins, sorts, and group by.

The reducers are on the other end of the shuffle stage, in order to process the data partitions generated by the mappers. The reducers have the operation of applying transformations to the partitioned data before writing it out.

Figure 8-1 illustrates this processing flow, in which data is input and processed in the mappers, sorted and shuffled, and then sent to the reduce processing stage before being written to storage.

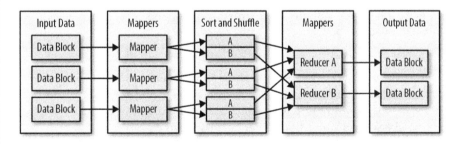

Figure 8-1. MapReduce processing flow

Although MapReduce provides a stable and reliable tool for distributed data processing, drawbacks have led to the introduction of new engines that are increasingly replacing MapReduce as the tool of choice. Here are some of the most prominent of those drawbacks:

Lack of DAG management

As you can see in Figure 8-1, the processing sequence of a MapReduce job is a map job followed by a reduce job (although for completeness, in some cases it makes sense to eliminate the map or reduce phase to perform a task); you can do only a single sort and shuffle and then you must write back out to disk. If you need to do something more complex, like two joins, you need to implement multiple MapReduce jobs that run one after the other.

I/O overhead

MapReduce was designed at a time when memory was still expensive, so it made extensive use of disk. A MapReduce job will need to read and write large volumes of data to and from disk and different stages of processing. This has a large effect on the performance of jobs and contributes to the relative slowness of MapReduce.

Startup times

Mappers and reducers can take many seconds to spin up, and after they've finished their task, the processes are terminated.

Difficult to code

The main interface to implementing MapReduce jobs is via Java applications, which provides obstacles to nonprogrammers. Additionally, understanding how to express a problem as a MapReduce job can be challenging. Although abstractions provide more-intuitive interfaces to MapReduce, generally speaking, using MapReduce as a processing engine requires knowledgeable and experienced developers.

Heavy deployment model

Deploying a MapReduce job will often require transferring a large Java Archive (JAR) file to a cluster node for execution.

Although you likely won't see MapReduce being used to implement new processing jobs, you'll find these patterns of mappers, shuffles, and reducer repeated in distributed computing.

Even though MapReduce was powerful at the time because it was one of the only distributed execution systems available, it was difficult to use for the reasons we just enumerated. The level of effort was considerably greater than trying to implement something like SQL on a traditional relational database.

The answer to these problems, at the time, was Apache Hive, which provided a SQL abstraction over MapReduce and supported the creation of DAGs over MapReduce. Even though Hive was slow and not suited for interactive queries, it was widely popular because it made the power of MapReduce accessible to SQL developers.

Internal DAG management

MapReduce is increasingly being replaced by more modern processing engines like Apache Spark or Apache Flink. One of the properties that ties these tools together is that they all have an execution engine that supports the creation of DAGs. This support for DAG creation within the engines provides the ability to more easily implement efficient and complex processing jobs.

Even Hive, which started as an abstraction over MapReduce, has been extended to support engines that can support the creation of more-complex DAGs; for example, Apache Tez, which provides a framework for supporting the creation of DAGs to process data.

Compute Isolation

Our next category for consideration is how the system manages compute isolation; this is essentially defining how the system manages allocation of resources for executing tasks. We can break this into the following options:

Node-level isolation
>   In this option, only a single job task runs on a node.

Container level
>   In this option, we have one job running within a container, but multiple containers can exist on a node.

Task level
>   The execution engine manages multiple tasks within its processes.

These options are supported by different systems, so let's talk through each of them and discuss where and how they fit based on different use cases.

Node-level isolation

This again is where a node is constrained to running a single task associated with a job at a time. Node-level isolation became popular with the rise of the cloud offerings such as Amazon Elastic MapReduce (EMR). In this model, a user would spin up an EMR cluster to execute a job and then terminate the cluster on job completion.

The benefit this provides is not having to worry about other jobs competing for resources. A downside is the amount of time to spin up the cluster instances. Another potential downside is low resource utilization; the chances are high that not all resources on nodes would be 100% used while executing a job.

Container-level isolation

There are a couple of different dimensions to container isolation; one is containers running within a cluster resource manager and job scheduler such as YARN or

Mesos. The other is the increasing use of solutions like Docker and Kubernetes that provide virtualization services that allow multiple containers to run on a single server.

Although container technologies like Docker and Kubernetes might be integral components in deployment architectures, they likely won't affect your choice of processing engines, because these technologies will be agnostic to the software deployed inside them.

Selection of processing engine will likely be tied more closely to a cluster resource manager, though; for example, engines like Spark and MapReduce are generally run within a system like YARN or Mesos in order to manage resources. Running Spark within YARN, for example, allows YARN to control the allocation of tasks to available containers.

Task-level isolation

Task-level isolation, which is supported by a number of modern processing engines (for example, Apache Impala, Apache Presto, or Apache Spark), allows for different workloads to run with single processes in the system. This might mean that processes need to switch between tasks and might create the possibility of resource conflicts. However, this also can increase the efficiency of jobs, for example, by removing the need for spinning up processes to execute tasks.

Hidden isolation

It should also be mentioned that in some cases considerations around isolation are essentially hidden from you. This will be the case when using some cloud-based tools like Amazon Athena and Amazon Lambda. This is also being referred to now as *serverless computing*.

Isolation considerations

Selecting the isolation type is dependent on several factors, including the following:

Number of jobs versus budget
> If your company has the money and node-level isolation is acceptable, it's generally the easiest option.

Limited spending
> If budget is limited, a multitenant architecture will likely be required, which will probably mean container isolation. For example, a Hadoop cluster running multiple jobs using YARN.

Strict latency requirements
> When latency requirements are low, a system that supports task-level isolation might be optimal.

Cloud deployments
> If you're deploying to the cloud, isolation choices might already be made for you when you use specific cloud services, as we mentioned.

Performance

Although the performance of an engine in executing your jobs is important, it's necessary to look beyond just fast engines that can execute specific workloads. What's important is understanding the performance of a tool in executing your use cases. In some cases, a tool might be fast at executing certain queries, but can have problems executing more-complex queries requiring multiple joins, and so forth. Consider the attributes of the following tools:

Presto
> Provides a fast execution engine but can run into issues if queries don't fit into memory.

Spark
> Fast, but doesn't currently facilitate use of external tools such as business intelligence tools in a multitenant environment.

Hive with the Tez engine
> Fast, but you still need to deal with other components in the Hive architecture such as the Hive Metastore.

Additionally, your choice of tool might be driven by things like a decision to move jobs from an existing system. For example, you might have existing data models and queries deployed in a Teradata system. Many Teradata applications will use colocated joins based on indexed columns, which allows for fast joins across many tables on a single join key. If this is a data model you have used for years and you have thousands of jobs built based on this, you will have little chance of success moving to an execution engine that doesn't offer an optimization in a similar way. In this case, a replacement for colocated indexes might be bucketed and sorted joins in Hive. On the other hand, other engines might not be able to support this type of model. Again, the important point here is that your choice of tools will be driven by considerations beyond just raw performance. It's also important to keep in mind that performance will be based on your use cases, so it's best when possible to run tests based on your specific workloads.

Fault Tolerance

In general, we can bucket processing frameworks into three categories of fault tolerance:

- No fault tolerance

- Executor recovery

- Full job recovery

Let's look at each of these categories in more detail. One thing you'll see repeated when we discuss fault tolerance in distributed systems is the trade-off between recovery and performance.

No fault tolerance

The first category of fault tolerance we discuss is no fault tolerance; in other words, systems that offer no options for recovery in the eventuality that jobs fail. This might sound undesirable, but in fact, it can make sense when you prioritize the performance of jobs. Not having the overhead of recovery means an engine can focus on pure speed of query execution, which provides benefits for ad hoc and analytical queries, which are generally queries that complete and quickly return answers to users. Even in the case of failure, it's generally the case that these engines will be fast enough to restart the query execution and return answers quickly.

On the other hand, these tools are not well suited for long-running tasks such as Extract, Transform, and Load (ETL) jobs, but these are not the types of workloads these engines target.

Tools that fall under this category include Impala and Presto. These engines are designed to efficiently serve analytical queries and are well suited for integration with business intelligence (BI) and analytical tools. The typical query for Impala or Presto will complete within seconds. The odds of node failure within that time frame are low, and even if node failure occurs, the time to reprocess the query is low enough to not be a concern.

One thing to note, though, is the increase in performance in fault-tolerant engines such as Spark SQL. Even though Spark SQL might not equal the performance of Impala or Presto, it can be close enough to meet your performance requirements and provide the benefits of recovery in the case of failure. Note that at the time of writing, the Spark SQL architecture has deficiencies that make it less suitable for use in serving BI and analytical tools in multiuser scenarios.

Executor recovery

This classification of recovery is for systems like Hive, MapReduce, and Spark. Systems that provide this type of fault tolerance offer recovery if you lose an executor process, as long as you don't lose the driver process. In other words, you can lose one or more tasks that are executing a job, but as long as the driver process is still running, jobs won't fail.

Take, for example, a long-running job such as a k-means clustering job. In a typical job executing a k-means algorithm, the job will iterate over the data many, many times, and this job can take tens of minutes to hours to complete, depending on the number of iterations, number of dimensions, and data size. Clearly if you're partly complete with a job that's been running for minutes or hours, the expense of having to completely restart the job on failure is very high. Fortunately, with this type of recovery, the system can simply move the processing of a failed task to a new process and rerun that one task.

Figure 8-2 shows an example of a Spark job in which an executor fails. In this case, the output of tasks that have completed successfully can still be consumed, and the system just needs to reexecute the task that failed, rerunning any previous tasks that are required as input to the task that failed.

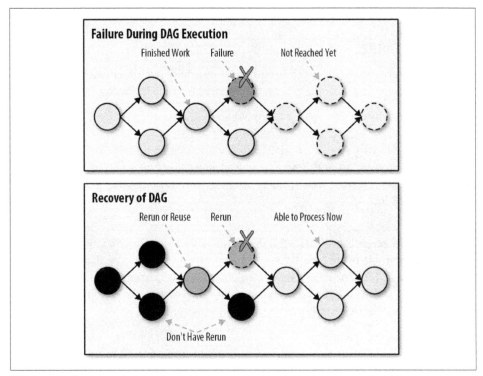

Figure 8-2. Recovery in a system that supports executor recovery

As you'd expect, this type of recovery adds complexity to a processing engine, but provides benefits for long-running jobs, particularly when there are SLAs associated with those jobs.

There can also be limitations in the case of executor recovery. Taking Spark as an example, the state of the processing is maintained by the driver, so without a high-availability configuration, if the driver process is lost, the job is lost and will need to be restarted from the beginning.

Full job recovery

Full job recovery is most commonly found in processing engines that also serve as streaming engines. Engines that fall into this category include Flink, Spark Streaming, and Kafka Streams, as well as other modern streaming engines. You can imagine this is important because a strong requirement of a streaming job is the ability to stay running for long periods of time, even weeks or months. With those types of time frames, failure is inevitable, including failures related to the driver.

The mechanisms that these systems use is beyond the scope of this chapter, but in general, these engines will support recovery through things like checkpointing. This does involve additional overhead such as the configuration of persistent storage to store checkpoints, not to mention the overhead to read and write checkpoints.

Interaction Model

In general, interaction with execution engines normally occurs either through code, SQL, or a combination of both. We can group tools into the following categories:

Java Database Connectivity (JDBC)/Open Database Connectivity (ODBC) access
This allows for SQL access just like a normal relational database, which allows you to use third-party BI or analytic tools for interacting with the engine. Most tools that support an SQL interface will support this type of access; for example, Hive, Impala, Presto, Cassandra, or Spark SQL (although with limitations mentioned earlier).

SQL through code
Allows the execution of SQL queries, similar to a standard relational database. Any of the tools in the previous category will almost certainly fit into this category as well. Most of these engines will also support extension via user-defined functions (UDFs). UDFs provide the ability to perform more-complex processing that's not natively supported by the particular engine.

Non-SQL declarative models
Available tools provide a declarative programming interface similar to SQL. These interfaces are intended to provide the ability to express complex programming tasks, but with an easier interface than needing to write code. A good example of this model is Apache Pig, which provides a declarative programming language called Pig Latin. Although these engines have been useful for implementing some use cases, with the introduction of engines like Spark, there seems to be declining usage of these tools, which likely also means less resources and developer experience. It's probably best to carefully evaluate the usage of these tools for new development.

Programming code

These are engines that require developers to implement processing in a programming language such as Python, Java, or Scala. Common examples of engines that fall into this category include Spark, MapReduce, or Flink.

The picture is somewhat complicated by the fact that some engines that fall into the programming code category can be used with higher-level abstractions such as a SQL abstraction. For example, Hive actually compiles queries into code to be run by an execution engine such as MapReduce or Spark.

The decision of which engine to use will be determined by your use cases and the experience of your team. For example, if processing is being implemented by analysts, the likely tool will be an engine that provides a SQL interface such as Hive. Jobs that can't easily be expressed in SQL will likely be developed in a coding engine such as Spark or Flink.

Batch and/or Streaming

Our final category is the type of workloads that the engine is targeting. Generally speaking, we can break this into engines that are suited for batch processing jobs; that is, jobs that run processing over large numbers of records, either periodically or on a one-time basis. These jobs often take minutes to hours to complete. Stream-processing engines, on the other hand, are designed to continuously process incoming events and will generally produce results with much shorter time periods.

The classic example of a batch-processing engine is MapReduce, which is suitable for jobs that need to run processing over large blocks of records. MapReduce was followed by engines like Spark, which although more efficient than MapReduce, is still targeted at long-running batch jobs.

Stream-processing engines, on the other hand, are designed for more real-time processing of data. These engines will perform continuous processing on incoming streams of events, returning results in seconds or subseconds. Examples of these types of engines are Spark Streaming, Kafka Streams, Apache Storm, and Apache Heron.

You'll note that Spark was mentioned in both batch and streaming categories. This is because the Spark processing model can support both batch and stream processing, although with some small implementation and deployment differences. Flink is another example of a tool that can support both models, again with some small differences. There are advantages to using a tool that can support both models:

- You need to learn only one programming interface to implement both batch and stream processing jobs.
- The ability to reuse code between both batch and stream jobs.

- Reduced complexity in deploying and managing applications.

The decision between batch or job processing will likely come down to the specific use case being implemented. For ETL or machine learning applications, the answer will almost certainly be batch. Stream processing is suitable for jobs that need closer to real-time reactions to incoming data; for example, in a fraud detection system, or an application that needs to run calculations over data windows.

A couple of features that typify stream-processing engines are good to be aware of. The first feature is the way processing flows are implemented. Some tools like Apache Storm or its successor Apache Heron follow a *topology model*. Similar to a DAG, a topology model is an abstraction to express a graph for executing transformations on data. More recent engines like Spark use a DAG model. The main difference is in how applications are coded using the different models. You can express most problems with either model, so this might not be a primary consideration in choosing a tool.

The other primary feature is the way the tool manages the state of processing. Some tools like Storm manage processing state in memory and require additional work to manage state persistently; for example, on disk. Other tools like Spark provide better support for state management, which can provide better support for failure recovery for cases in which a process is lost, along with its associated data in memory.

Data Processing over Time

To put this all in some perspective, let's explore how data processing management systems have evolved over the past several decades. Although the details might be debatable, Figure 8-3 illustrates this evolution. Looking at this from the data management perspective, we've seen the following:

- We start with the introduction of the relational database in the 1970s (single-node RDBMS). These early databases typically ran on a single server, and managed only an amount of data that could fit on those servers.
- The need for management of larger data sizes led to the introduction of distributed databases, typified by the Massively Parallel Processing (MPP) databases such as Teradata and Vertica.
- As data volumes and types continued to grow, eventually even these MPP systems became technically and economically impractical for many workloads, leading to the introduction of new data management systems such as Hadoop, Cassandra, and so on.

Along with changes in how data is managed and stored, we've seen corresponding changes in how that data is processed:

- Data integration requirements such as moving and transforming data led to the growth in ETL tools to help implement and automate these processes.
- As with data storage, the increase in volume and variety of data sources over time led to the introduction of new frameworks to perform efficient parallel processing of data; for example, MapReduce and Spark. These frameworks allowed ETL processing to be moved from traditional data management systems and proprietary tools to these new open source distributed systems.

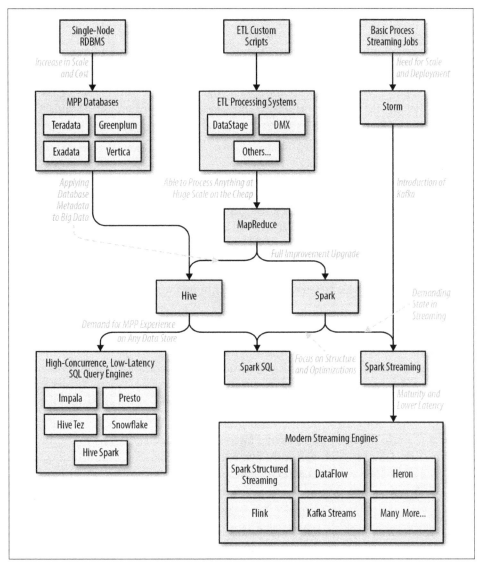

Figure 8-3. The evolution of data processing

As part of the growth of open source data management tools, we've seen the introduction and evolution of systems to perform processing of streaming data. An early example of these systems was Apache Storm, which was followed by Spark Streaming. There are now a number of powerful tools available for performing near-real-time processing of streaming data, which previously would require expensive, proprietary solutions.

The need for reliable and effective storage and transformation has remained a constant over this time. The big difference now is the dramatic change in scale; as we mentioned, we've gone from databases on a single node to systems that can support thousands of nodes and consume millions to billions of records each day. This scale would have been unthinkable decades ago.

Additionally, we've gone from a world with a few major providers of data management software to one in which we have an abundance of choices, including the large vendors like Oracle and IBM as well as the open source projects and vendors. The introduction of cloud providers further increases the data management landscape.

Summary

In this chapter, we provided some guidelines for evaluating processing frameworks based on characteristics that typify parallel processing engines. These characteristics include the following:

- How the engine supports definition of execution plans; specifically, support for defining a DAG when implementing applications. Support for defining DAGs is an important consideration when implementing more-complex processing flows.

- The isolation model within which an engine can be executed. This can have an impact on the performance of a tool, particularly within a multitenant environment.

- The performance characteristics of a tool. Considerations around performance go beyond just the raw speed of an engine. For example, a particular engine might run queries quickly but might not be suitable if you require fault tolerance.

- And speaking of trade-offs between performance and fault tolerance, different engines have different mechanisms for responding to failure of jobs. Some tools provide strong support for continuing a job when part of it fails, whereas others require complete restart of a job on failure.

- How users interact with the engine. Can they execute SQL queries, or does the tool require writing code? This consideration can be important, depending on on the background and skills of your team.

- And finally, whether the tool is designed for batch or streaming workloads (or in some cases both). In general, these two models are suitable for different use cases, so this will be important when selecting an engine to implement a specific use case.

Ultimately, your selection of processing engine will be influenced to a great degree by the skills on your team, in combination with the preceding list. For example:

- You have a team of analysts who need to be able to execute efficient analytical queries. In this case, a tool like Impala or Presto is likely a good choice.
- You have developers skilled in implementing ETL jobs using SQL. In this case, you need an SQL-based engine that supports fault tolerance, so Hive or Spark SQL will likely be better choices than Impala or Presto.
- You have Java or Scala developers who need to implement complex machine learning algorithms. Here, a tool that can implement sophisticated batch jobs like Spark or Flink will likely be good candidates for evaluation.

Our hope is that you'll be able to use the guidelines presented in this chapter in combination with your use cases to identify suitable tools to implement the processing needs of your data projects.

Index

throttling records, 8
throughput, 21
times to live (TTL), 69
topology model, 162
toxic personalities, 53
transactions
    snapshot versus serializable isolation, 114
    transactional locking, 22
transformations, 129, 146
tunable consistency, 108-110
typographical conventions, x

U

User Defined Functions (UDFs), 160

V

version management
    embedded code and, 6
    for interfaces, 76
    strategy for, 7
Vertica, 162

About the Authors

Ted Malaska is Director of Enterprise Architecture at Capital One. Previously, he was Director of Engineering of Global Insights at Blizzard, helping support titles such as *World of Warcraft*, *Overwatch*, and *Hearthstone*. Ted was also a principal solutions architect at Cloudera, helping clients find success with the Hadoop ecosystem, and a lead architect at the Financial Industry Regulatory Authority (FINRA). He has also contributed code to Apache Flume, Apache Avro, Apache Yarn, Apache HDFS, Apache Spark, Apache Sqoop, and many more. Ted is a coauthor of *Hadoop Application Architectures*, a frequent speaker at many conferences, and a frequent blogger on data architectures.

Jonathan Seidman is a software engineer on the Cloud team at Cloudera. Prior to that, he was a solutions architect at Cloudera working with partners to integrate their solutions with Cloudera's software stack. Previously, he was a technical lead on the big data team at Orbitz Worldwide, helping to manage the Hadoop clusters for one of the most heavily trafficked sites on the internet. He's also a cofounder of the Chicago Hadoop User Group and Chicago Big Data, coauthor of *Hadoop Application Architectures*, technical editor for *Hadoop in Practice*, and has spoken at a number of industry conferences on Hadoop and big data.

Colophon

The animals on the cover of *Foundations for Architecting Data Solutions* are the buffalo weaver (*Dinemellia dinemelli*) and the baya weaver (*Ploceus philippinus*). Both are members of the Ploceidae family of which there are numerous species. Birds of this family are known colloquially as weavers for the way they weave together their nests from natural materials like sticks and leaf fibers.

Buffalo weavers are native to Africa and get their name from their habit of feeding on insects disturbed by the movement of the African buffalo. In addition to insects, buffalo weavers feed on fruits and seeds. They forage together in groups and are known to be highly social.

Baya weavers are found in India and southeast Asia, and are distinguished by their tube-shaped nests, which they build hanging from tree branches. Like buffalo weavers, baya weavers forage together in groups. They often feed on grains and rice, and so are classified as an agricultural pest in parts of India.

Many of the animals on O'Reilly covers are endangered; all of them are important to the world. To learn more about how you can help, go to *animals.oreilly.com*.

The cover image of the buffalo weaver is from *Wood's Animate Creation* and the cover image of the baya weaver is from *Cassell's Natural History*. The cover fonts are URW Typewriter and Guardian Sans. The text font is Adobe Minion Pro; the heading font is Adobe Myriad Condensed; and the code font is Dalton Maag's Ubuntu Mono.

Learn from experts.
Find the answers you need.

Sign up for a **10-day free trial** to get **unlimited access** to all of the content on Safari, including Learning Paths, interactive tutorials, and curated playlists that draw from thousands of ebooks and training videos on a wide range of topics, including data, design, DevOps, management, business—and much more.

Start your free trial at:

oreilly.com/safari

(No credit card required)